UCHICAGO **Consortium**
on School Research

I0157652

RESEARCH REPORT   MAY 2022

Standards-Driven Instructional Improvement

Lessons Learned in Chicago

Elaine M. Allensworth, Sarah Cashdollar, Amy Cassata, and Julia A. Gwynne
with Jeanne Century, Debbie Leslie, Lisa Sall, and Nick Tallant

TABLE OF CONTENTS

ACKNOWLEDGEMENTS

We are very grateful to the Math and Science department at the Chicago Public Schools, especially Jessica Mahon, for their partnership and input on this work. We would like to thank a number of colleagues who gave input on different versions of this report, including Lisa Sall, Briana Diaz, John Easton, Jessica Tansey, and David Stevens, and members of our Steering Committee who gave feedback on project findings at various stages of the work. We are also very grateful to the anonymous reviewers of the articles on which most of the findings reported in this report are based. The research reported here was supported by the Institute of Education Sciences, U.S. Department of Education, through Grant R305A1600162 to the University of Chicago. The opinions expressed are those of the authors and do not represent views of the Institute or the U.S. Department of Education.

We thank the Consortium Investor Council that funds critical work at the Consortium: putting the research to work, refreshing the data archive, seeding new studies, replicating previous studies, and making research equitable. Members include: Brinson Foundation, CME Group Foundation, Crown Family Philanthropies, Lloyd A. Fry Foundation, Joyce Foundation, Lewis-Sebring Family Foundation, Mayer & Morris Kaplan Family Foundation, McCormick Foundation, McDougal Family Foundation, Polk Bros. Foundation, Spencer Foundation, Steans Family Foundation, Square One Foundation, and The Chicago Public Education Fund. The Consortium also gratefully acknowledges the Lewis-Sebring Family Foundation, whose operating grant supports the work of the UChicago Consortium.

Cite as: Allensworth, E.M., Cashdollar, S., Cassata, A., Gwynne, J.A., Century, J., Leslie, D., Sall, L., & Tallant, N. (2022). *Standards-driven instructional improvement: Lessons learned in Chicago.* Chicago, IL: University of Chicago Consortium on School Research.

This report was produced by the UChicago Consortium's publications and communications staff: Jessica Tansey, Managing Director of Research Communications, and Jessica Puller, Senior Communications Strategist.

Graphic Design: Jeff Hall Design
Photography: Eileen Ryan; Unsplash (Clayton Robbins & Louis Reed)
Editing: Jessica Tansey and Jessica Puller

05.2022/PDF/jh.design@rcn.com

Executive Summary

The Common Core State Standards in Mathematics (CCSS-M) were released in 2010 with a goal to improve critical thinking skills and prepare all students to thrive in college, careers, and as informed citizens.[1] The Next Generation Science Standards (NGSS) followed in 2013. Most states across the country adopted the standards, which brought ambitious new targets for both students and teachers, but there has been little evidence about whether instructional practices improved.

Existing studies on the CCSS-M have focused almost exclusively on changes in average test scores across states as a whole—and those results have shown a mix of slightly positive, negative, and no changes. They tell us little about which strategies for implementing the standards might have been effective, as they do not account for the variation that exists across schools and districts within those states. They also tend to focus on one part of the standards—the content standards (the content students should learn at each grade level), and say little about outcomes from the practice standards, which provide goals around cognitively demanding math and science proficiencies (e.g., ability to reason abstractly, critique arguments, construct explanations) that cut across content areas.[2]

Making deep changes in instructional practice is challenging, and policymakers often underestimate what it takes to realize large-scale change.[3] New standards by themselves cannot raise student achievement—they depend on the work of districts, schools, and teachers to interpret the standards and effectively shift instructional practice.[4] The standards describe what students should know and be able to do, but how to achieve instructional change was largely left up to districts.[5] This study provides a summary of what happened in one district—Chicago Public Schools (CPS)—as district staff and educators worked to promote change in instructional practices in math and science aligned with the new standards.

Chicago's plan placed a strong emphasis on the practice standards—working to change the ways students experienced math and science instruction. The district used a teacher-leader model in which multiple teachers from each school participated in workshops and professional learning communities around the standards, and then those teachers were tasked to support school-wide change with their colleagues. The district also provided an online repository of resources, called the Knowledge Center, which included instructional materials, curriculum recommendations in math, and materials to support school-wide collaboration and sharing. Using districtwide surveys of students in grades 6-8, conducted annually from 2011 through 2018; annual data on student achievement; surveys of teachers in the 2014–15 and 2017–18 school years; and interviews of teacher-leaders, school principals, and district officials, this study examines the results of district efforts to implement the CCSS-M and NGSS standards.

---

1 Windschitl & Stroupe (2017); Haag & Megowan (2015).

2 See http://www.corestandards.org/Math/Practice/ and https://www.nap.edu/catalog/13165/a-framework-for-k-12-science-education-practices-crosscutting-concepts

3 Hatch (2013); O'Day & Smith (2016).

4 Toch (1991); Tyack & Cuban (1995).

5 Desimone et al. (2019).

It is not possible to fully separate the effects of standards implementation strategies from the many other district policies that were enacted at the same time—the changes could have been due to these other policies, or to the combination of all of them.[6] Changes in science and in high school math instruction that were found here are consistent with successful implementation of the standards, but may have resulted from other policies enacted simultaneously. Of note, in the middle grades, it was possible to conduct analyses that specifically examined the influence of professional development around the standards in math on student achievement. Those analyses found significantly more improvement in math instructional practices and student achievement in schools with more extensive professional learning around the standards than in other schools in the district.

Key Findings

Math and science instruction improved in Chicago during the years of standards reform, based on student survey reports of their classroom experiences. Students reported more frequently engaging in standards-aligned instructional practices over time, compared to similar students in the same schools in earlier years. Math instruction improved more at schools serving students from the least economically resourced neighborhoods than at other schools, and differences in the frequency with which high- and low-achieving students engaged in standards-aligned practices in their math classes diminished considerably. In science, there were improvements in instruction across all schools, with changes similar regardless of school characteristics or student achievement level.

Professional learning—defined broadly to include teacher collaboration, coaching, and workshops—was the most important support strategy for instructional change. Teachers who reported engaging in more professional learning around the standards also reported more frequently using standards-aligned practices in their classes. Professional learning showed a much larger relationship with teachers' practices than teachers' use of a recommended core curriculum in math, or their use of instructional resources. School-based professional learning, including collaboration and coaching, was an important part of professional learning around the standards, and showed a stronger relationship with practices than workshops alone.

In interviews, teacher-leaders identified collaboration with knowledgeable colleagues as the factor that led to the most substantial changes in instruction in their school. At many schools, multiple teacher-leaders from the same school attended professional development around the standards together. Some school principals were also able to participate in learning communities around the standards with their teacher-leaders. Having multiple colleagues training and working together helped create collective efficacy and buy-in so that teachers could experiment with new practices with support from others.

Collaboration around instructional improvement required dedicated time, multiple people with expertise, buy-in, trust, and administrator support. Through interviews, teacher-leaders described the many ways they tried to enact instructional change in their school. They felt the greatest change came from collaborative work, but the degree to which they could collaborate with others around instructional change depended on other conditions in the school, including administrator support, staff commitment to changing practice, trusting teacher relationships, dedicated time to work on instruction, and knowledgeable colleagues who could be true collaborators. Much of teacher-leaders' work involved building these supports to have better conditions for supporting collaboration.

Instructional resources provided by the district were helpful for implementing strong practices when they were instruction-ready, while other resources showed a null or negative relationship with practices. In math,

---

6 For example, the district implemented a new teacher evaluation system (REACH), and a new discipline policy around the same time.

teachers and principals described instruction-ready resources such as Math Talks and MARS tasks[7] as "game changers," and teachers who used those resources were more likely to implement standards-aligned practices. They noted that it was easy to see how the materials fit with different standards, and that students enjoyed using them. In science, the resources available at the time data were collected for the study (2017–18) mostly focused on the scope and sequence of topics in the content standards, and required teachers to figure out how to apply them in the classroom. A greater use of those resources was associated with less frequent use of standards-aligned practices. Using a district-recommended, CCSS-M-aligned curriculum also did not show an independent relationship with practices, after taking into account that teachers who participated in more professional learning around the standards also were more likely to use a recommended curriculum.

Instructional practices mattered for student achievement. In schools where students and teachers reported frequently using standards-aligned practices in their math and science classes, there were stronger gains on assessments than in schools where few students or teachers reported frequent use of standards-aligned practices. Among students who initially had low- or average- test scores, gains on the NWEA-MAP in math were stronger in sixth and eighth grade at schools with more standards-aligned instruction, as were gains on the ninth-grade PSAT in mathematics. There were also larger gains on the science strand of the PSAT/SAT in high schools with more standards-aligned practices in science classes.

Overall, this study shows that large-scale instructional change is possible when key supports are in place. Changing practices mattered for students overall, improving average learning gains, and mattered most for students who did not already have high achievement, thus improving educational equity. The district put resources towards the goal of changing instructional practices, providing workshops, networks, and curricular resources, and worked with university partners to develop an implementation strategy that emphasized innovating, collaborating, and sharing in schools. Those elements of implementation seemed to be most crucial for change. The district strategy of sending multiple teacher-leaders to professional learning, in particular, allowed for productive collaboration in schools around standards-aligned instruction. However, this required time from teachers, and in some schools, teacher-leaders and principals said they did not have sufficient time to dedicate to instructional change given many other competing priorities. Instructional resources helped teachers modify their instructional practices when designed in a way that made them very easy to use, and the combination of high-quality resources with professional learning showed the strongest relationship with standards-aligned instructional practices. At the same time, there was considerable variation across schools in teachers' participation in professional learning and the degree to which teacher-leaders could promote change in their schools. School and district leaders might consider how they could support instructional change broadly by ensuring each school has multiple teacher-leaders receiving training on standards-aligned instruction, broad buy-in for instructional change, and sufficient time to collaborate.

---

7   MARS (2012).

Introduction

Illinois adopted the Common Core State Standards (CCSS) in 2013, and the Next Generation Science Standards (NGSS) one year later. The CCSS-M and the NGSS not only called for changes to what is taught through content standards but also required changes in how math and science are taught, laying out what students should be able to do with the content they learn though the standards for mathematical practice in the CCSS-M and the scientific and engineering practices in the NGSS. The CCSS-M, for example, called ing on which implementation strategies districts used. The limited research on how student outcomes have changed in response to the new standards have shown mixed results, with math scores failing to rise nationally, after falling in the first year the CCSS-M were widely implemented. As a result, some policymakers are at a point where they have given up on the standards, with the former U.S. Secretary of Education proclaiming, "Common Core is a disaster. And at the U.S. Department of Education, Common Core is dead."[13]

The new standards were intentionally constructed to allow for flexibility in implementation across districts and schools. Therefore, we can expect the effects of the new standards on student outcomes to vary widely, depending on which implementation strategies districts used.

---

on teachers to move from asking students for an answer to asking students to form arguments, defend their positions, and explain their problem-solving process.[8] NGSS are equally ambitious and required teachers to change their practice from teaching facts to challenging students to investigate phenomena, form arguments and conclusions, and engage in productive discourse.[9]

Teachers implementing new reforms must balance the demands of time and energy to shift practice with their many other responsibilities.[10] Standards-aligned instruction has proven challenging nationally, especially in terms of the practice standards. While teachers report making changes to their teaching,[11] they have found it difficult to engage students in the conceptual processes that the CCSS-M and NGSS demand.[12] The new standards were intentionally constructed to allow for flexibility in implementation across districts and schools. Therefore, we can expect the effects of the new standards on student outcomes to vary widely, depend-

Walking away from significant investments in the Common Core standards may be premature without understanding how they have been implemented and influenced instruction and student learning. While the standards were adopted by states, how to implement them in schools has been largely left up to districts.[14] Districts could support instructional change through many different mechanisms, which would influence whether or not they were successful. Most of the research on the CCSS-M examines whether there were state-wide changes. This study provides a very different way of looking at the results of standards implementation, taking an in-depth examination of what happened in the middle and high school grades in one large district—Chicago Public Schools (CPS). In Chicago, we were able to leverage a large array of data to get a detailed look at the outcomes of standards implementation across the district—data which are largely not available in other places.

---

8   Common Core State Standards Initiative (2020).
9   Shernoff et al. (2017); Windschitl & Stroupe (2017).
10 Hess (1998).
11 Bay-Williams, Duffett, & Griffith (2016); Kane, Owens, Marinell, Thal, & Staiger (2016); Opfer, Kaufman, & Thompson (2016).
12 Friedrichsen & Barnett (2018); Opfer et al. (2016); Tekkumru-Kisa, Schunn, Stein, & Reynolds (2019).
13 Downey (2018, January 16).
14 Desimone et al. (2019).

This report summarizes the findings of a multi-year study to learn about the district's plans for implementing the CCSS-M and NGSS, how the plans were enacted by schools, and whether there were changes in students' experiences and achievement in their math and science classes in the middle and high school grades. To do this, researchers interviewed district leaders and staff, as well as university partners that worked with the district to develop implementation plans, to understand the various mechanisms through which the district was promoting instructional change. Findings from those interviews were used to construct survey questions to discern how teachers' experiences corresponded with the district plans. The questions were then embedded in the teacher version of the *5Essentials* Survey, a districtwide survey administered annually to both students and teachers. Researchers also interviewed a number of school principals and teacher-leaders in the 2017–18 and 2018–19 school years to understand in more depth how they viewed and experienced the process of standards implementation. In addition, researchers looked at whether there were changes in students' reports of their experiences in their science and math classes from before and after standards implementation, based on annual student responses to the *5Essentials* Survey. Researchers also analyzed the relationships between instructional practices with student achievement.

This report summarizes findings, addressing questions that include:

1. What was the Chicago plan for standards implementation?
2. Did students' reports of instruction in math and science classes change with implementation of the standards?
3. Which implementation supports were associated with greater use of standards-aligned instructional practices?
4. Were standards-aligned instructional practices related to learning gains?
5. What did teachers say were barriers to instructional change, and what was helpful for changing practice?

Data Used for This Study

This report summarizes findings from four more detailed manuscripts, listed below. Data used in our analyses included:

Interview data with district leaders and university partners on the district plan. To understand and document the district plans for standards enactment, researchers conducted eight interviews: six district leaders (the directors of the Science and Mathematics departments, and two specialists on each team), and two university partners who worked closely with central office staff to develop plans around standards reform.

Interview data with school principals on school supports and barriers. Researchers interviewed 12 principals across five networks in the 2017–18 school year to understand school leaders' perspectives of standards implementation, including the key supports and barriers influencing their school's implementation of each set of approaches.

Interview data with teacher-leaders on their experiences changing their own instruction and promoting change in their schools. The research team conducted in-depth interviews with 16 teacher-leaders in the fall of 2018, including seven math teacher-leaders and nine science teacher-leaders representing 13 CPS schools located across 11 of the 13 CPS geographic networks. Of these schools, six served students in grades 9-12, four were in grades pre-K-8, and three were in grades 7-12.

Survey data on teachers' experiences. Survey responses of teachers to the annual 5Essentials Survey were used to discern teachers' experiences around standards implantation, as well as the instructional practices used in their classrooms. In spring 2018, the survey contained questions about both the CCSS-M and the NGSS. Response rates among teachers were and 80 percent in 2018, however, to decrease the burden on survey respondents, teachers who taught both math and science were randomly assigned to answer questions about only one subject, leading to survey responses from about 60 percent of the teachers who taught either subject.

Survey data on students' experiences. Student survey responses on the annual 5Essentials Survey were used to capture their experiences in their math and science classes, including the frequency in which they engaged in standards-aligned practices. Student survey response rates ranged from 74 percent to 83 percent for the surveys administered in the spring of 2011 through 2018.

Administrative data on student achievement and background. Administrative data provided information on student test scores in math and science.

Corresponding Manuscripts:

1. **Allensworth, E., Cashdollar, S., & Gwynne, J. (2021)**
Improvements in math instruction and student achievement through professional learning around the Common Core State Standards in Chicago. *AERA Open, 7*(1), 1-19.

2. **Cassata, A., & Allensworth, E. (2021)**
Scaling standards-aligned instruction through teacher-leadership: methods, supports, and challenges. *International Journal of STEM Education, 8*(39).

3. **Allensworth, E., Cashdollar, S., & Cassata, A. (2022)**
Supporting change in instructional practices to meet the Common Core Mathematics and Next Generation Science Standards: How are different supports related to instructional change? *AERA Open.*

4. **Century, J., Cassata, A., & Leslie, D. (2018, April 14)**
Implementing standards initiatives in mathematics and science within a large, urban district: Principal perspectives on supports and barriers. Paper presented at the American Educational Research Association Annual Meeting, New York, NY. (Available from author)

CHAPTER 1

Implementation Plan

What was the Chicago plan for standards implementation?

After Illinois adopted the CCSS-M in 2013, the CPS Department of Mathematics launched a multi-year effort to support teachers' transition to the new standards (see Figure 1). The first teacher-leader workshops on the math standards were offered in 2013, which schools could participate in on a voluntary basis. By 2015, the district expanded teacher leader workshops on the CCSS-M to all schools in the district. The district took a similar approach to support the transition to the NGSS. After the science standards were released in 2013, the district developed teacher-leader workshops that were fully implemented by 2016. Their focus was on helping teachers modify their instructional practices so that students would develop the procedural and conceptual understanding called for by the practice standards.

The district's professional learning program emphasized "high quality" instruction, and creating equitable, student-centered learning environments through the Teaching for Robust Understanding (TRU) Framework. The district partnered with local universities to develop and provide content for professional development sessions in math, which was also informed by Charlotte Danielson's Framework for Teaching. When the state adopted the NGSS, the district took a similar approach to implementation in science.

The district also provided resources to support instruction through a website called the "Knowledge Center." These included a list of recommended K-12 math curricula aligned to CCSS-M, as well as standards-aligned lessons, instructional units, and student activities for implementing strong practices in mathematics. During the years of this study, instructional resources were very limited in science. The Knowledge Center also housed tools for conducting peer observations and sharing formative feedback. Professional development sessions often helped teachers use the materials provided by the Knowledge Center and the resources it contained to support professional learning within schools.

A primary feature of the professional learning program for both math and science was a teacher-leader model. Teacher-leaders had opportunities to attend workshops and participate in professional learning communities. They were expected to develop their own classroom practice to better align with the goals of the standards and support colleagues in their schools to make instructional improvements. The district also offered a number of voluntary standards-focused workshops and opportunities for professional development and collaboration that teachers could attend if they were not designated teacher-leaders. Teachers

FIGURE 1

Timeline of Standards Implementation in Chicago

2010
Common Core State Standards in Mathematics Released

2013
CCSS-M Workshops Begin in CPS

2015
Full CCSS-M Implementation in CPS; Expanded Profesional Learning

2010   2011   2012   **2013**   2014   2015   **2016**

2013
Next Generation Science Standards Released

2016
CPS Fully Implements NGSS

became leaders not through a change in their formal roles or responsibilities, but through their participation in professional learning (PL) experiences that positioned them as sources of expertise. In math, two or three teachers from every school were designated teacher-leaders who could attend Teacher Leader Institutes (TLIs). There were fewer resources available learning with other teachers and administrators in their building by collaborating to review student work, inviting a peer into their classroom to observe, observing another person's classroom and providing constructive feedback, or engaging others in informal conversation about what they were learning. By providing aligned professional development opportunities, resources,

---

"This [strategy] was going to be about high-quality instruction. Then if the materials changed, the standards changed, if anything — the assessment — changes, it doesn't matter because this is still good teaching."
— CPS District Leader

---

for NGSS implementation, with the result that the science TLI program was limited to about one-quarter of schools. However, the district sponsored other standards-focused science PL opportunities for all teachers, and for particular teacher groups based on grade level or disciplinary content area, developing "pockets" of science teacher-leaders in addition to those trained through the TLIs. There were also workshops for school leaders and network chiefs, and some schools were part of "deep support" networks, where they received extra opportunities for professional learning through university partnerships. In math, schools in "deep support" networks had opportunities for school teams that included both teachers and administrators to participate in professional learning together.

High-quality instructional practices were a major component of the TLIs across all years, and TLIs in 2014–15 and later years also included topics around how to share learning at the school level (e.g., working with adult learners), and supporting professional learning with colleagues through public practice. Following the TLIs, teacher-leaders were expected to share their

and professional communities of practice, teacher-leaders were being prepared to work to improve their own instructional practices, and to collaborate with colleagues to promote instructional change in the school. The goal was to see instructional change aligned to the practices in the CCSS-M and NGSS (see Figure 2).

Teachers' and principals' reports of their experiences were consistent with the district plan. On the 2017–18 *5Essentials* Survey, teachers reported engaging in the types of professional learning that were intended by the district plan, and their most frequent sources of professional learning around the standards came from interactions with school colleagues. In both the middle grades and the high school grades, and in both math and science, many teachers reported frequently participating in collaborative planning time and classroom observations with other teachers. More teachers reported that "developing high-quality instructional practice" was a substantial emphasis of their professional learning around the standards than other topics (see the Supplemental Appendix for details).

FIGURE 2
Chicago Theory of Action for Standards Implementation

Professional Learning and Knowledge Center Resources → Teacher Leaders → Standards Aligned Instructional Practices → Collaboration with Colleagues → Students and Teachers Report Instructional Change

The principals interviewed for this study reported that the workshops and some of the materials for supporting instructional change were helpful for supporting changes in instructional practice among their teachers. At the same time, they varied in the degree to which they felt there were enough opportunities for professional learning to support the changes that were needed, and there were limitations to how well they felt their school could implement the teacher leader model. More information about principals' perspectives and the district plans are available in the paper, **Century, Cassata, & Leslie (2018, April 14).** Teacher-leader perspectives from interviews are described further below.

Key Components of Chicago's Implementation

- **Emphasis on practice standards**, including high-cognitive demand tasks, promoting student discourse, using formative assessments.

- **Network-based teacher-leader model:** A system for developing teacher-leaders with the expectation that these leaders should spread knowledge, resources, and instructional practices to other teachers in their schools.

  - District-supported courses, workshops, institutes, and professional learning communities building capacity to implement high-quality instruction.

  - Emphasis on experimentation and sharing among teachers as opposed to a uniform approach.

  - Emphasis on creating equitable, student-centered learning environments through the TRU Framework.

  - Training for multiple teachers from the same school to build a professional community around instructional change.

- **PL Experiences for some network and school administrators:** District-supported courses, workshops, institutes, and professional learning communities building capacity to support high-quality, standards-aligned math and science instruction.

- **Knowledge Center:** District-supported website housing district-developed and/or curated tools and resources promoting high-quality, standards-aligned instruction.

  - Tools for peer observations and formative feedback.

  - **Math:** A list of recommended K-12 curricula aligned to the CCSS-M.

  - **Math:** Instruction-ready materials to support standards-aligned math practices, such as Math Talks and MARS tasks, tied to professional development.

  - **Science:** Resources during the time of this study were in the early stages, mostly scope-and-sequence documents; fuller sets of resources added in later years.

CHAPTER 2

Instructional Practices

Did students' reports of instruction in math and science classes change with implementation of the standards?

Each year, students in grades 6-12 answer questions on the annual *5Essentials* Survey about their experiences in their math and science classes. Questions about how often they engage in specific instructional activities have been asked on the surveys since before the state adopted the new standards. Over time, since the adoption of the standards, students have reported engaging more frequently in practices aligned with the standards in their math and science classes than before the standards were adopted.

In math, there was a small increase in students' reports of practices aligned to the standards in the first year that workshops were offered around the CCSS-M (2012–13), and middle grade students reported much more frequently doing standards-aligned practices in the first year of full implementation (2014–15) and in each of the subsequent years (see Figure 3). High school students reported engaging in standards-aligned practices in their math classes much less frequently than students in the middle grades, but their reports also increased beginning in 2015–16, and continued to increase through the 2017–18 school year. A prior study found that elementary teachers were more enthusiastic and engaged in preparing for the CCSS-M than high school teachers, and student reports of their instruction are consistent with those patterns.[15]

Equity in students' experiences in their math classes improved over time. Prior to the adoption of the CCSS-M, students with high achievement reported much more frequently engaging in standards-aligned practices than students with low-achievement. These differences narrowed considerably over time. All students reported engaging in standards-aligned practices slightly more frequently after CCSS-M implementation than they did in earlier years, but the changes were largest among students with low test scores. In fact, by 2017–18, in schools where teachers reported extensively participating in professional learning around the CCSS-M, low-achieving students reported more frequent use of the practices in their math classes than high-achieving students did in schools where teachers reported limited professional learning around the standards (see the Supplemental Appendix and Allensworth, Cashdollar and Gwynne, 2021 for details).

Student Survey Questions about Standards-Aligned Practices in Math

In your MATH class this year, how often do you do the following:
(Never, Rarely, Sometimes, About half the time the class meets, About every time the class meets)

- Write a few sentences to explain how you solved a math problem.
- Explain how you solved a problem to the class.
- Write a math problem for other students to solve.
- Discuss possible solutions to problems with other students.

- Apply math to situations in life outside of school.
- Solve a problem with multiple steps that takes more than 20 minutes.
- Write a few sentences to explain how you solved a math problem.

---

15 Cowhy & Gwynne (2017).

FIGURE 3

Students Engaged in Standards-Aligned Math Practices More Frequently Over Time

Student reports of practices in their math classes, controlling school fixed effects and student backgrounds

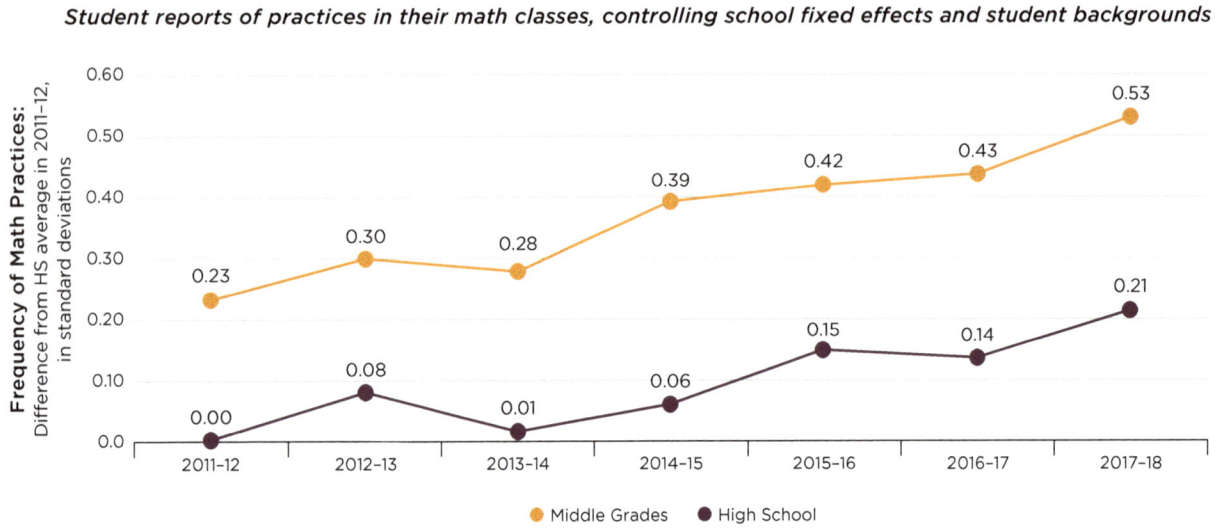

Note: Values are based on statistical models that controlled for school fixed effects and student characteristics including race, gender, socioeconomic status, grade level, and the type of math class in which students were enrolled. Average scores on the math practices measure were significantly different from 2011–12 in all years with the exception of high school reports in 2013–14.

The district provided extra professional learning opportunities for schools in particular networks, and they prioritized schools serving greater numbers of students with low test scores and students who were economically disadvantaged. Consistent with these efforts, there were larger improvements in mathematics instructional practices in schools serving students living in neighborhoods with the highest poverty rates (**see the Supplemental Appendix for details**).

In science, students also reported more frequently engaging in scientific practices over time. The survey questions asked of students about activities in their science classes were consistent with NGSS goals around active engagement through hypothesis/question generation, writing about science, and making interpretations with data, but they were less strongly aligned with the NGSS than the questions in math were aligned with the CCSS-M. In the middle grades, students' reports of science practices increased over time, showing the largest increases in the same years as seen with changes in math practices, 2012–13, 2014–15, and 2017–18 (**see Figure 4**). In the high school grades, the largest increase in practices reported by students occurred in the first year of full NGSS implementation, 2015–16, with another substantial increase in 2017–18.

As seen in math, middle grade students reported more frequently engaging in scientific practices than high school students, and the increases were larger in the middle grades than in high school.

Changes in math and science instructional experiences were significant, even after considering other potential influences. Using statistical models, the study examined whether the changes in students' reported instructional experiences could have been due to changes in the background characteristics of the students attending the middle grades (e.g., different students attending CPS over time), students taking different types of classes, or changes in which schools students enrolled in over time (e.g, students moving into newly-opened schools). The changes in instructional experiences remained statistically significant.

Other district policies and practices changed simultaneously in the district with standards reform, including the implementation of the REACH teacher evaluation system, new discipline and social-emotional learning policies and supports, and changes to district accountability systems. It is not possible to completely disentangle the effects of the different policies on student outcomes. We can say that students increasingly experienced standards-aligned instruction in

In your SCIENCE class this year, how often do you do the following:
(Never, Rarely, Sometimes, About half the time the class meets, About every time the class meets)

- Generate your own hypotheses
- Use evidence/data to support an argument or hypothesis
- Find information from graphs and tables
- Use laboratory equipment or specimens
- Write lab reports

FIGURE 4

Students Engaged in Standards-Aligned Scientific Practices More Frequently Over Time

Student reports of practices in their science classes, controlling school fixed effects and student backgrounds

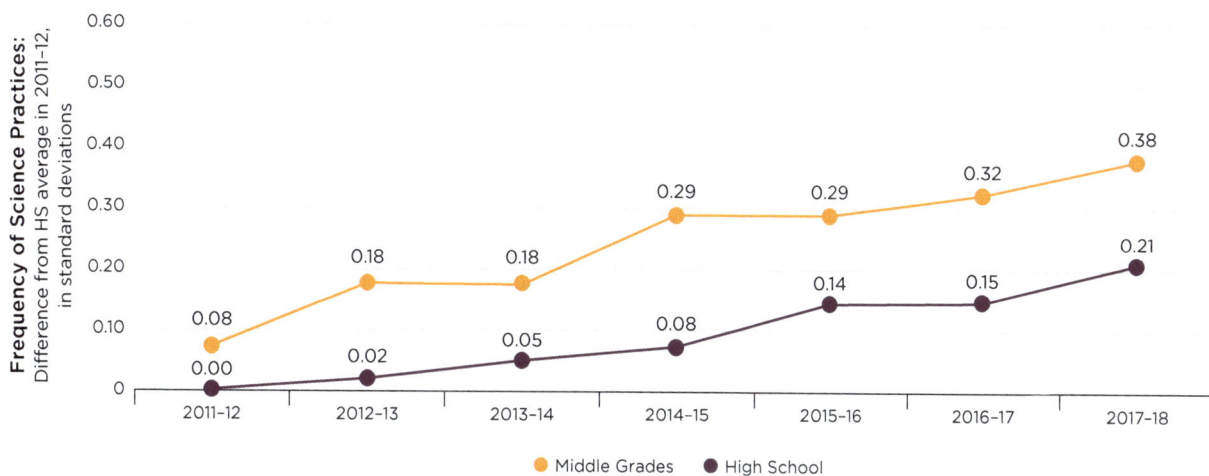

Note: Values are based on statistical models that controlled for school fixed effects and student characteristics including race, gender, socioeconomic status, grade level, and the type of science class in which students were enrolled. Average scores on the science practices measure were significantly different from 2011–12 in all years with the exception of high school reports in 2012–13.

their math and science classes during the period of time when standards implementation and all of the other policy reforms occurred. In addition, in the case of math instruction in the middle grades, we conducted analyses that specifically showed that professional learning around the CCSS-M was related to the improvements instruction and student outcomes **(see the box titled *Professional Learning and Middle Grade Math Achievement* on p.16).**

Professional Learning and Middle Grade Math Achievement

In the first year of CCSS-M implementation, 2014–15, there was considerable variation across schools in the degree to which middle grade math teachers reported participating in professional learning (PL) around the standards. This allowed researchers to isolate changes in students' reports of their instructional experiences, and changes in student achievement, based on the degree of teacher participation in professional learning around the standards in the school. Details of the study are available in **Allensworth, Cashdollar and Gwynne (2021)**.

There were significantly larger improvements in students' reports of the frequency of their engagement in standards-aligned math practices after CCSS-M implementation (2014–15) in schools where teachers reported more PL around the standards than in schools with limited standards-focused PL. There were also larger improvements in multiple measures of math achievement. Overall, annual gains on the MAP increased by about 0.06 standard deviations more in schools with extensive PL than schools with limited PL. Math GPAs increased by about 0.13 GPA points more in schools with extensive PL than schools with limited PL. Math course pass rates increased by 3-4 percentage points more among students with low test scores (in the bottom third of students) in schools with extensive PL relative to schools with limited PL around the standards, and improved by 1.5 percentage points among students with average achievement.

CHAPTER 3

Implementation Supports

Which implementation supports were associated with greater use of standards-aligned instructional practices?

Standards do not change instructional practices by themselves; improvements in instruction require investments in supports such as instructional materials and professional learning (PL). Knowing which supports are most helpful is important to discern the relative value of investing time and money into them. In this study, researchers examined the degree to which CPS teachers' participation in district-led standards-focused PL and use of district-recommended, standards-aligned instructional resources were related to their use of standards-aligned instructional practices as reported on the 2018 *5Essentials* Survey.

Teachers' instructional practices were more strongly related to their PL around the standards than to their use of a recommended core curriculum or other instructional resources. This was true in both math and in science, and in high schools and in elementary schools (**see Figure 5**). The more that teachers reported emphasis on CCSS-M/NGSS topics in PL, or the more frequent participation in PL opportunities around the standards, the more frequently they reported using standards-aligned math and science practices.

Both workshops and collaboration were related to stronger practices, although collaboration showed a stronger relationship. The combination of workshops and collaboration showed the strongest relationship. Furthermore, the relationship of professional learning with instruction was just as strong among teachers who reported many barriers to standards implementation as among teachers who reported few barriers.[16] Studies in other places have also found significant

relationships between professional learning around the standards and student instructional experiences and outcomes.[17]

Instruction-ready resources were related to standards-aligned instructional practices, while scope-and-sequence resources were not. Teachers who reported using supplementary materials available on the Knowledge Center in math also reported their students participating more frequently in CCSS-M-aligned math practices. These resources included MARS tasks and Math Talks, and teachers who reported using those resources also reported more frequent overall use of standards-aligned practices in their classes, especially in the middle grades (**see the Supplemental Appendix for more details on the use of Math Talks and MARS tasks**). The principals and teacher-leaders interviewed for the study also described the MARS tasks and Math Talks as extremely helpful for changing instructional practices (**see description below, and also Century, Cassata, and Leslie, 2018, April 14**).

Among science teachers, a greater use of supplementary resources from the Knowledge Center showed a negative relationship with NGSS-aligned practices. Even among teachers with substantial PL around the standards, a greater use of the Knowledge Center resources was not associated with stronger practices. As discussed below, these resources required teachers to figure out how to modify their instruction, making it more difficult to plan instruction, rather than making it easier for them to enact new practices. Since the time data were collected for this study, the district has expanded the resources available for science teachers.

---

16 Teachers answered questions asking how much each of the following was a barrier to standards implementation: Not enough time to collaborate with other math teachers; being held accountable for student assessments that are not aligned with CCSS-M_M (math only); inadequate professional development on math/science instructional practices; students' inadequate preparation in prior grades; lack of administrator

support for changing instructional practice; students' wide-ranging instructional needs; too many other competing job demands; not enough time during class to get through the lesson.

17 Kane et al. (2016); Shernoff, Sinha, Bressler, & Schultz (2017); Tyler, Britton, Iveland, Nguyen, & Hipps (2018).

FIGURE 5

Professional Learning Showed Stronger Relationships with Instructional Practices than Core Curriculum or Other Recommended Resources

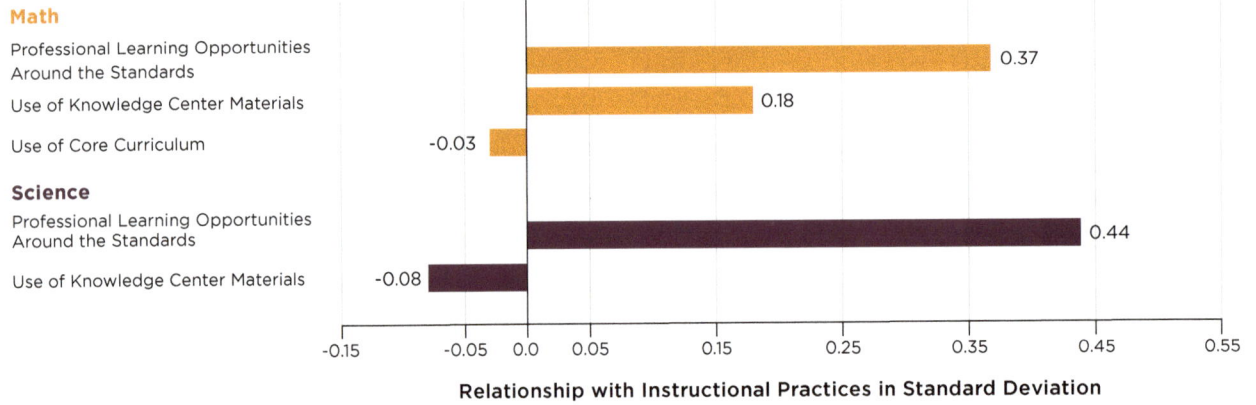

*Relationships of implementation supports with teachers'
instructional practices, net of use of other implementation supports*

Math

Professional Learning Opportunities Around the Standards — 0.37

Use of Knowledge Center Materials — 0.18

Use of Core Curriculum — -0.03

Science

Professional Learning Opportunities Around the Standards — 0.44

Use of Knowledge Center Materials — -0.08

Relationship with Instructional Practices in Standard Deviation

Note: Relationships come from coefficients of a model that predict teachers' reports of their use of standards aligned instructional practices in spring 2018 with their reported use of each of the implementation supports, controlling for teacher characteristics (grade level, teacher leader status) and school characteristics (average student social status, neighborhood poverty, average prior math score, and students' reports of instructional practices in 2017). Analysis is based on responses from 2,033 math teachers in grades 6-12. All coefficients except use of core curriculum are significant at p<0.05.

The contrast that exists in the first several years of standards implementation is useful for considering the impact that different kinds of resources can have—resources that are designed to improve instruction might have the opposite or null effect if they increase the workload on teachers rather than making it easier for them to enact new practices.

Curriculum use alone was insufficient for improving instructional practices. The Knowledge Center provided a list of recommended curricula for CCSS-M instruction. Among teachers with similar participation in PL around the standards, those who reported using a core curriculum did not report a greater use of standards-aligned practices than those who used a different curriculum. The combination of more PL and use of a core curriculum was not related to stronger practices than PL alone. Studies outside of Chicago also did not find significant effects on student outcomes from changing to a new textbook in response to standards, or using a curriculum that was designed pre- vs. post-CCSS-M.[18]

Further details of the analysis of implementation supports and teachers' instructional practices are available in **Allensworth, Cashdollar, and Cassata (2021)**.

---

18 Kane et al. (2016); Blazar et al. (2019).

CHAPTER 4

Learning Gains

Were standards-aligned instructional practices related to learning gains?

More frequent use of standards-aligned instructional practices should lead students to have a deeper understanding of mathematical and scientific concepts, but teachers and school administrators might wonder whether that deeper learning is reflected on the standardized assessments for which they are held accountable. Researchers looked at whether there were differences in test gains in schools where either teachers or students reported high overall use of standards-aligned practices relative to schools with less frequent use of standards-aligned practices. Statistical models compared similar students in similar schools—controlling for students' prior year test scores, demographic characteristics (race, ethnicity, gender, socioeconomic status), and school characteristics (prior year average test scores, racial composition, average socioeconomic status of students).

There were significantly higher gains on standardized assessments in schools where either teachers or students reported more frequently engaging in standards-aligned practices in their math. Figure 6 shows the degree to which learning gains were different from the district average at schools where many teachers reported using standards-aligned practices in 2017–18, relative to the district average.

In math, in sixth and eighth grade, gains were significantly higher on the NWEA-MAP in schools where more teachers reported using standards-aligned practices. Among students with low prior test scores, gains were also higher on the ninth-grade PSAT in math in high schools where more teachers reported using standards-aligned practices in their math classes. On average, students' scores increase by about 0.30

FIGURE 6

Schools Where Teachers Reported Frequent Use of Standards-Aligned Practices Showed Stronger Gains on Assessments Than the District Average

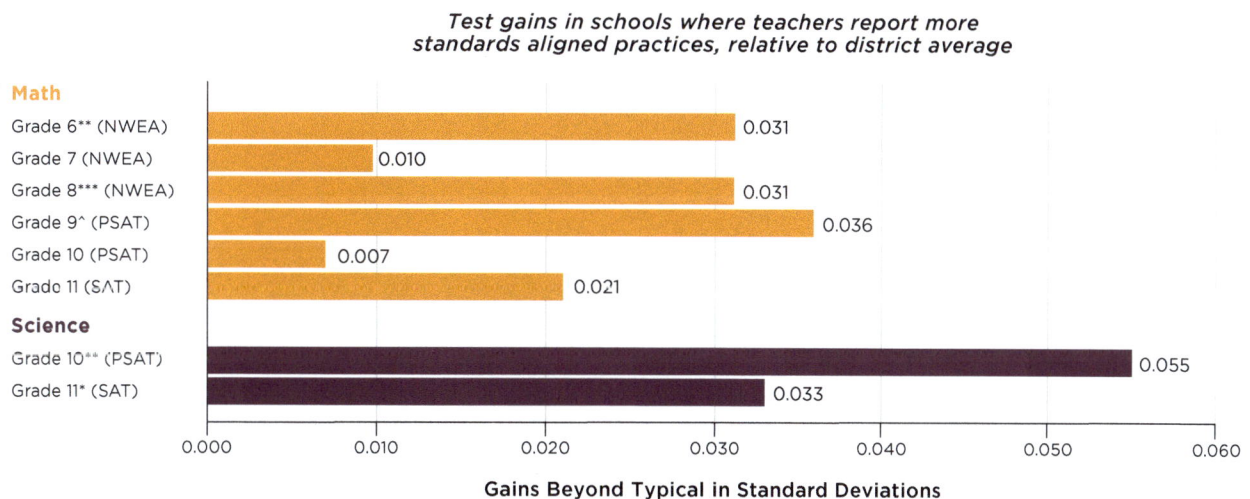

Test gains in schools where teachers report more standards aligned practices, relative to district average

Math
- Grade 6** (NWEA): 0.031
- Grade 7 (NWEA): 0.010
- Grade 8*** (NWEA): 0.031
- Grade 9^ (PSAT): 0.036
- Grade 10 (PSAT): 0.007
- Grade 11 (SAT): 0.021

Science
- Grade 10** (PSAT): 0.055
- Grade 11* (SAT): 0.033

Gains Beyond Typical in Standard Deviations

Note: **$p<0.01$, ***$p<0.001$, ^not significant overall, but significant at $p<0.01$ among students with below-average prior achievement. Gains are based on the NWEA-MAP in grades 6-8, the PSAT in grades 9 and 10, and the SAT in eleventh grade from 2017 to 2018. Science scores are based on the SAT/PSAT science strand. These come from a model that controls for student's score in the same subject test the prior year, with the exception of ninth grade where student's eighth-grade NWEA-MAP score in math is used as the prior score. The models also control for students' race, ethnicity, economic background, special education status, and school economic composition (mean poverty and mean social status), racial composition, and average test score in the prior year in the school. Standards-aligned practices are measured by teachers' responses to questions about how often their students did particular standards-aligned activities. About 60 percent of teachers answered these questions in the survey. Improvement in gains compares a school one standard above the mean to the mean.

standard deviations a year, so the differences suggest gains were 10 percent higher in schools with greater use of standards-aligned instructional practices than typical in an average school, and 20 percent higher than in a school with low frequency of standards-aligned practices. Teacher reports were based on only about 60 percent of math teachers in a school—this might lead to an underestimate of the relationship between test gains and practices. Using student reports instead of teacher reports of instructional practices in a school as the measure of instructional practices, we find that the relationships are larger, and significant in seventh and ninth grade, as well as sixth and eighth grade (**see the Supplemental Appendix for details, as well as Allensworth, Cashdollar & Cassata, 2022**).

Tenth- and eleventh-grade math gains were not significantly related to either student or teacher reports on instructional practices. These differences might reflect very different practices in tenth and eleventh grades among math teachers in geometry, algebra II, and pre-calculus classes, such that there is less consistency by school.

The degree to which a school as a whole used stronger instructional practices was most consistently associated with stronger math gains for students with low and average achievement, than for students with high achievement. In fact, learning gains for students with high prior test scores were not significantly related to school-wide instructional practices at any grade level.

This could be because students with high achievement are more likely to encounter standards-aligned instructional practices in their classrooms than other students, even in schools with weaker instruction overall. For students with low prior test scores in sixth and eighth grade, gains at schools with strong instructional practices were especially large—20 percent larger than the district average and 40 percent larger compared to schools with infrequent use of practices. **See the Supplemental Appendix and Allensworth, Cashdollar & Cassata (2022) for specific results.**

In science, schools where teachers reported using more NGSS-aligned practices showed larger gains on the science strand of the PSAT and SAT. The science strand of the PSAT/SAT combines items from across the subtests in reading, writing, and math to produce a science strand score. For example, they include in the science score questions from the reading section that ask students to delineate the experimental process described in a text, analyze data from research or a graphical figure, or determine which conclusion is supported in a study's findings.[19] These gains were also about 10-20 percent larger in schools with more frequent standards-aligned instructional practices than an average school, and 20-40 percent larger relative to schools with weak or inconsistent standards-aligned practices. Unlike in math, the size of the gains was similar among students with different prior test scores.

---

19 College Board (2015).

CHAPTER 5

Barriers & Boosters

What did teachers say were barriers to instructional change, and what was helpful for changing practice?

A few years after states adopted the Common Core State Standards, about two-thirds of math teachers across the country felt that they did not have a high level of preparation to teach the new standards—especially the practice standards—and were particularly concerned about their preparation to support students with a range of abilities.[20] Similarly, the most common barriers to standards implementation identified by CPS teachers on the 2018 *5Essentials* Survey were around students' wide-ranging instructional needs and students' prior preparation. Across the country, the majority of teachers implementing the NGSS also reported the need for additional professional development.[21]

In interviews, Chicago teacher-leaders described students' preparation as a barrier in terms of their ability to engage in open-ended tasks without a clear answer, more so than their knowledge of particular content or skills. Teachers believed their students felt uncomfortable engaging in mathematical and scientific practices to investigate problems and build conceptual understanding of core ideas. Math teachers explained that students were used to being taught procedures and then told whether or not they got the right answer. Under the new standards, students became frustrated with the need to persevere in problem-solving and construct their own explanations. As one high school math teacher said, "*I think that it has been difficult for our students to make that transition. They're very accustomed to asking the question, 'Is this the right answer? How do I get this? I don't know how to do this.'*" Science teachers also reported that students struggled with the transition from being instructed about content to constructing their own explanations, insisting "You're the teacher, tell me." Because student-led problem-solving could be time-intensive, teachers reported it was difficult to help students with pre-existing knowledge differences catch up to grade-level content. Teachers also found it difficult to adjust to variation in the amount of time different students needed to construct explanations, which posed problems for classroom management.

Over one-half of survey respondents also reported too many competing demands was a moderate or major barrier to standards implementation, and this came out as an issue in teacher leader interviews. Both math and science teachers felt stretched in a number of different directions, reporting that there were simply "not enough minutes in a day" to make all the instructional changes they envisioned around the standards on top of their other district and school responsibilities. Several teachers reported that their colleagues, especially veteran teachers, were hesitant to invest too much of their already-limited time into aligning instruction to standards that they thought may or may not be replaced within a few years. In science, high school teachers struggled to balance students' need for instruction aligned to science AP and SAT subject tests. Because there was no district science assessment, teachers felt strongly pushed to prioritize responsibilities other than aligning instruction to the NGSS. Even when additional professional learning (PL) opportunities were made available to them, some teachers reported not having time to participate as much as they wanted to.

Teacher-leaders identified collaboration with knowledgeable colleagues as most critical for instructional change. Teacher-leaders highly valued what they learned from the PL experiences provided by the district. They felt they received support as they developed and

---

20 Hamilton et al. (2016); Swars & Chestnut (2016); Kane et al. (2016); Makkonen & Sheffield (2016); Scholastic & the Bill & Melinda Gates Foundation (2014).

21 Haag & Megowan (2015).

tried out new techniques from the university partners and informal education institutions that were providing professional development. PL communities provided opportunities for ongoing collaboration with other expert teachers in their district networks, and some teachers also continued to engage with Central Office staff after a PL session had ended. These relationships provided continued access to resources and strategies for supporting standards-aligned teaching and assessment.

Teacher-leaders found it particularly beneficial when multiple staff members from the same school could experience PL together. As one teacher put it, *"It was nice to go with my colleagues because if I didn't understand something, I had someone there to help me understand how to roll out a lab or how to explain it or, you know, multiple resources to help support the learning."* Having multiple teachers who had attended professional learning also helped build momentum for change in their schools. Whether teacher-leaders had other colleagues who were working on instructional change made a big difference for their feelings of efficacy in shifting their instruction. Collaboration was necessary because the changes that teachers were being asked to make in their instruction were very difficult to implement. They also found it beneficial to make their practice open and transparent by documenting strategies and observing one another.

Teacher-leaders identified instruction-ready math resources as helpful. Math teacher-leaders noted that use of a district-approved curriculum helped build vertical alignment and horizontal alignment within schools, ensuring teachers covered all of the grade-level content standards by the end of the year. However, the instructional resources in the Knowledge Center (e.g., Math Talks and MARS tasks) were particularly helpful for changing instructional practices, allowing them to focus more on teaching than on figuring out what to do in each class. They appreciated both the large quantity of resources and their utility. Teacher-leaders felt students enjoyed the supplemental materials, which required them to persevere in problem-solving at an appropriate level of challenge. One teacher referred to the materials as "life changing," while a principal described them as a "game changer."

Unlike math teachers, science teachers felt they had to figure out how to build standards-aligned lessons, activities, and assessments with little guidance, which became a source of stress. In schools that had a science curriculum, teachers worked to supplement and align the curriculum to the NGSS, and some found it helpful to attend professional development offered by district partners on making these adaptations. Others reported that their school either had no curriculum, or had a curriculum that needed heavy modifications in order to align with the NGSS, and they built most materials from scratch. Given the major shifts in instructional design required by the NGSS and the lack of guidance in constructing aligned resources, this process was a heavy lift on top of teachers' other responsibilities.

Teacher-leaders' work to support school-wide change was facilitated by school-wide buy-in and structures for collaboration. In interviews, teacher-leaders discussed promoting instructional change in their schools through a number of different practices, such as advocating for change, providing individual support, inspiring others, sharing with colleagues, and working in collaboration. Consistent with the survey analysis, teacher-leaders believed the most large-scale changes in their schools occurred when teachers worked in collaboration, helping each other to create, implement, or reflect on shared projects, products, or practices. However, collaboration was only successful when teacher-leaders had other knowledgeable colleagues who could support each other, time for collaboration, trust among teachers who were collaborating, a commitment to change, and administrator support. **(See the Supplemental Appendix for definitions of teacher leader practices and school supports.)**

In schools where collaboration was encouraged and supported, teacher-leaders discussed the importance of having regular opportunities for exchanging resources, materials, and ideas to improve instruction throughout the school day. Much of this collaboration time was informal, taking the form of lunch meetings, consultations during prep time, or other check-ins throughout the day. But they also noted how important it was to have dedicated time for learning and adapting lessons, and for collaborating with other teachers, within the school day.

In some schools, teachers were able to point to school structures for collaboration that facilitated innovation and change in teachers' instruction. In other schools, the lack of structures for collaboration was seen as a barrier.

Much of the work of teacher-leaders involved building better supports and structures, rather than directly working on instruction, so that they and others could more effectively engage in collaboration and broad sharing of practices. For example, advocating for change could build administrator support, and broader staff commitment to instructional change. Providing individual support could lead to more trusting relationships, and more trusting relationships could lead other teachers to be inspired to learn more. **Figure 7** shows this process of building supports through practices, and facilitating practices through supports as a continual process of building. The practices do not have to build from one to the other; different teacher-leaders take different steps. However, the practices represented further to the right represent a deeper engagement around change in the school and require a broader range of supports. The stronger the supports in the school, the more time teacher-leaders could spend in those practices that directly influenced instructional change, rather than building the supports needed to engage in those practices.

For further details on teacher-leaders' reports of supporting instructional change, **see Cassata and Allensworth (2021).**

For further details on teacher-leaders' reports of supporting instructional change, **see Cassata and Allensworth (2021).**

FIGURE 7

Teacher-Leader Practices Were More Influential When They Had Broader Supports in the School

Model of teacher-leader practices and school supports

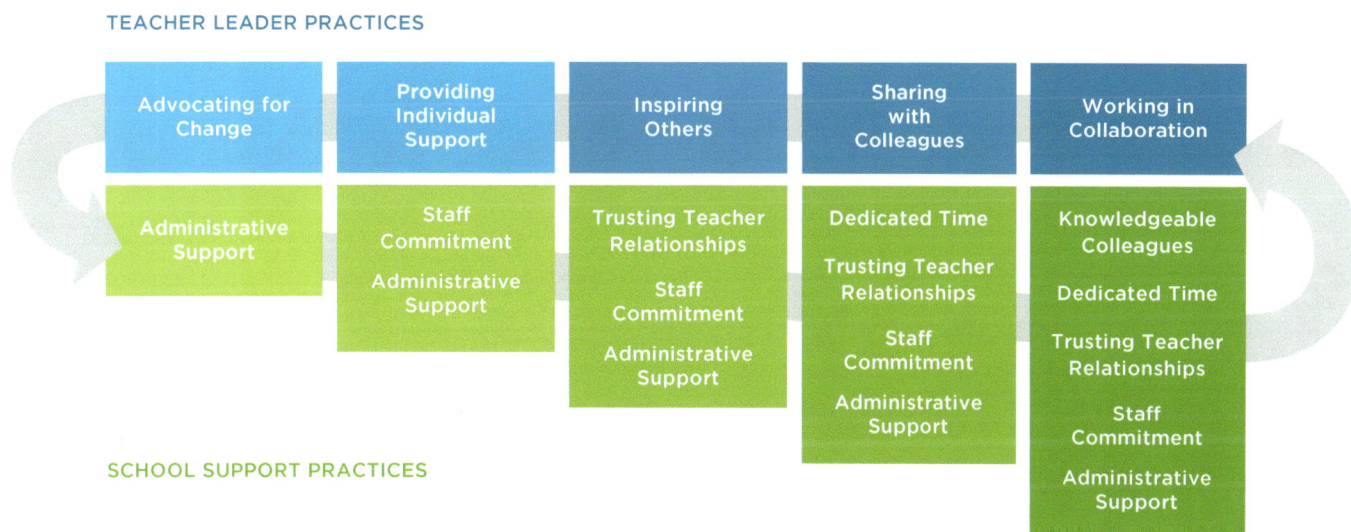

TEACHER LEADER PRACTICES

| Advocating for Change | Providing Individual Support | Inspiring Others | Sharing with Colleagues | Working in Collaboration |

| Administrative Support | Staff Commitment / Administrative Support | Trusting Teacher Relationships / Staff Commitment / Administrative Support | Dedicated Time / Trusting Teacher Relationships / Staff Commitment / Administrative Support | Knowledgeable Colleagues / Dedicated Time / Trusting Teacher Relationships / Staff Commitment / Administrative Support |

SCHOOL SUPPORT PRACTICES

Note: Practices further to the right reflect practices associated with more extensive change in the school, and generally require a broader range of supports to be successful. The stronger the supports at the bottom of the figure, the easier it is to engage in the practices above. Teacher-leaders may engage in different combinations of practices, not necessarily progressing from left to right. The three practices on the left can be done without administrator support, but administrator support makes those practices more likely.

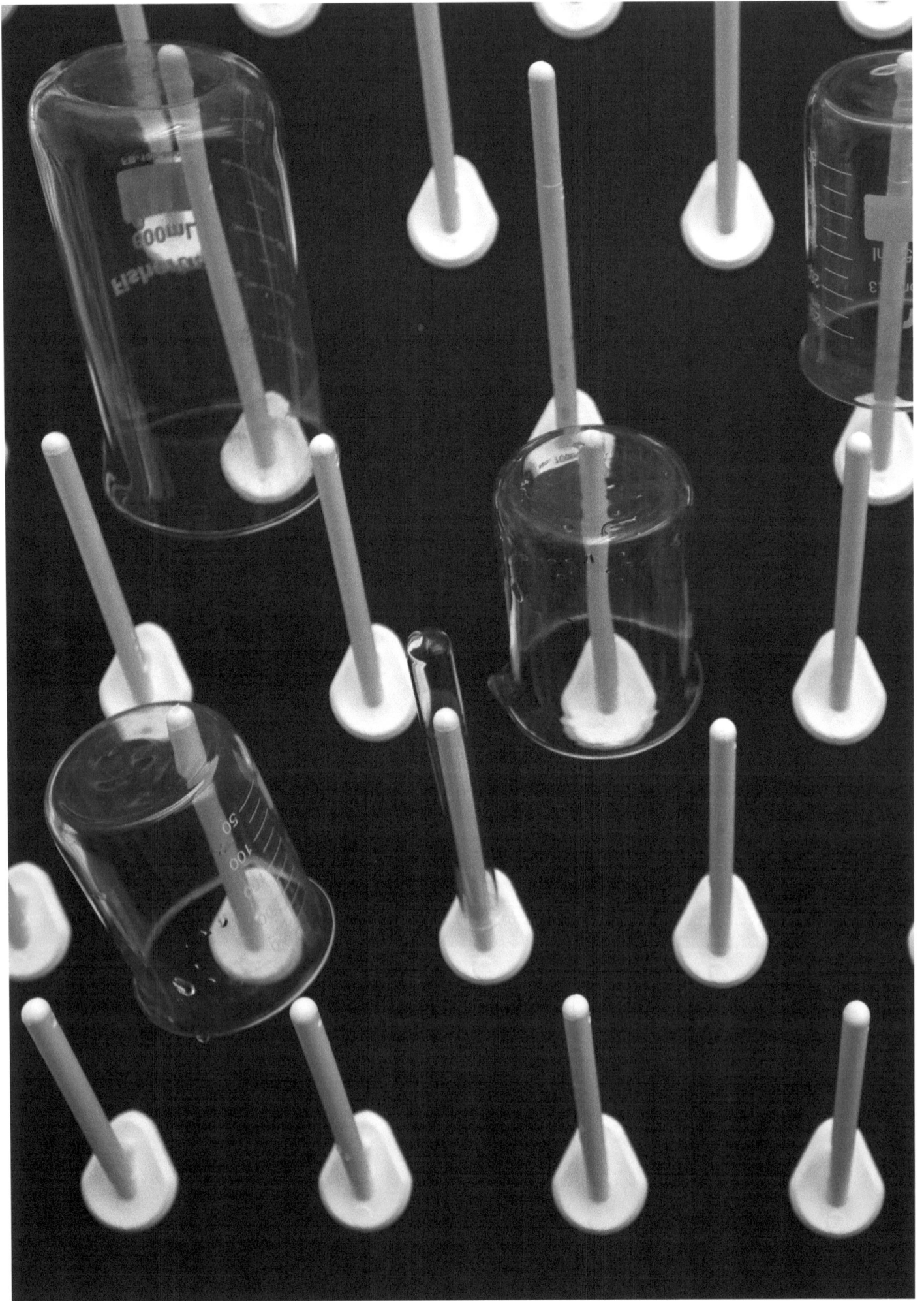

CHAPTER 6

Interpretive Summary

In the years since adopting the CCSS-M and NGSS, educators nation-wide have attempted to improve instruction and student learning using different standards implementation strategies, with little evidence of changes in student achievement overall. In Chicago, students increasingly engaged in instructional practices consistent with the new standards, and showed improvements in achievement.

We don't know whether there were other districts with successful implementation. The studies that exist in other places examine states as a whole, and focus on changes in the content standards, comparing the state standards before and after—not whether instruction actually changed, and whether it changed in ways other than shifting content. Importantly, improvements in instructional practices during this time in Chicago also could have been driven by other district changes; instructional practices improved from 2013 through 2018 during a time of multiple changes in district policies and supports. However, some of the decisions Chicago made around implementation deserve consideration for future efforts to implement instructional change.

It could be that CPS emphasized what ultimately matters most for student engagement and learning—high-quality instructional practices. It is possible that raising content standards without improving the quality of instruction does little to benefit students. Studies of prior policies intended to raise rigor in math classes have even found null or negative effects on low-achieving students.[22] Furthermore, a rigorous study of Common Core instruction that primarily focused on the content standards found no relationship between the alignment of teachers' instruction to the content standards and student academic gains.[23] Yet, as shown in this report, schools where either students or teachers reported more extensive instruction aligned to the practice standards showed larger annual gains on assessments than schools with less extensive use of those practices.

The district took an approach to teacher learning that allowed for experimentation and learning from failure. Rather than training teachers to implement curricula in a prescribed way, the district encouraged teachers to "try out" practices and share what worked with others. That can be frustrating for teachers and involves considerable uncertainty, but it also mirrors the goals of the Common Core State Standards for students—where students are presented problems and given support to find different solutions themselves. Instructional change involves numerous risks for teachers, and this process minimized the risks that are inherent in trying new practices, allowing teachers to do what they felt they could, based on support from their peers, and to build on what worked for them.

---

22 Allensworth, Nomi, Montgomery, & Lee (2009); Clotfelter, Ladd, & Vigdor (2015); Gamoran & Hannigan (2000); Simzar, Domina, & Tran (2016).

23 Polikoff & Porter (2014).

As a point of contrast, in 2006–09, CPS tried implementing a well-funded, ambitious strategy for instructional improvement in math, science, and English in 43 high schools with academically demanding, inquiry-based curriculum, technology-rich materials for implementation, common assessments, directed professional development, and intensive coaching (Instructional Development Systems, or IDS). While many teachers started off with enthusiasm about the new curriculum, they struggled to implement the challenging, student-centered tasks, and by the end of the year, many had reverted to traditional ways of teaching, and after three years the strategy was abandoned.[24] The history of education reform has many of these kinds of examples, of what has been called in improvement science as "implementing fast, learning slow," where full-scale implementation results in little learning or improvement.[25] The opposite is to "start small and learn fast," for example, through a networked improvement community that focuses on a common aim (e.g., new instructional practices), guided by an understanding of the problem, where implementers share knowledge as they learn from implementing what works in different contexts.[26] While not a formal networked improvement community, the district's implementation process had elements that were similar.

Training teams of teacher-leaders, or teachers and administrators together, was beneficial when it happened. Teacher-leaders found collaboration with colleagues to be extremely helpful if colleagues were knowledgeable, and there was a focus on improving instructional practices. When teacher-leaders reported having colleagues to turn to for support and knowledgeable feedback in this difficult work, they had more collective efficacy to support their own instructional change, and to support change throughout their school. Those teacher-leaders who were alone in their positions in their school had to spend much of their time trying to build supports for collaboration and sharing, rather than directly working on instructional practice.

The types of materials available to teachers mattered considerably. The availability of ready-to-use resources in math for promoting student discussion and problem-solving around multiple solutions made it easier for teachers to try new techniques. Materials that were not ready-to-use in science created more stress and meant less time to figure out how to support all students to engage in more difficult work. The TRU and Danielson frameworks integrated into the professional development around the standards further supported the emphasis on instructional practices and helped connect standards implementation with other district policies.

Administrator support was critical for promoting instructional change. Teacher-leaders not only needed their principals to support the goals of the standards, but to work with them to establish support structures around collaboration and learning, setting goals around instructional change in the school, and making sure there was dedicated time for professional learning and support for facilitating those meetings. Given the importance of administrative support in creating conducive school contexts for effective teacher leadership, districts might consider the best ways to involve principals and other administrators with decision-making authority in district-wide change initiatives, raising awareness of what makes for supportive school conditions for teacher-leaders to effectively facilitate instructional change.

24 Sporte, Correa, Hart, & Wechsler (2009).
25 Bryk, Gomez, Grunow, & LeMahieu (2015).
26 Bryk et al. (2015).

References

Allensworth, E., Cashdollar, S., & Gwynne, J. (2021)
Improvements in math instruction and student achievement through professional learning around the Common Core State Standards in Chicago. *AERA Open, 7*(1), 1-19. https://journals.sagepub.com/doi/full/10.1177/2332858420986872

Allensworth, E., Cashdollar, S., & Cassata, A. (forthcoming)
Supporting change in instructional practices to meet the Common Core Mathematics and Next Generation Science Standards: How are different supports related to instructional change? Under Review.

Allensworth, E.M., Nomi. T., Montgomery, N., & Lee., V.E. (2009)
College preparatory curriculum for all: Academic consequences of requiring algebra and English I for ninth-graders in Chicago. *Educational Evaluation and Policy Analysis, 31*(4), 367-391.

Bay-Williams, J., Duffett, A., & Griffith, D. (2016)
Common Core Math in the K-8 classroom: Results from a national teacher survey. Washington, DC: Thomas B. Fordham Institute.

Blazar, D.B., Kane, T., Polikoff, M., Staiger, D., Carrell, S., & Kurlaender, M. (2019)
Learning by the book: Comparing math achievement growth by textbook in six Common Core States. Cambridge, MA: Center for Education Policy Research.

Bryk, A.S., Gomez, L.M., Grunow, A., & LeMahieu, P.G. (2015)
Learning to improve: How America's schools can get better at getting better. Cambridge, MA: Harvard Education Press.

Cassata, A., & Allensworth, E. (2021)
Scaling standards-aligned instruction through teacher-leadership: methods, supports, and challenges. *International Journal of STEM Education, 8*(39).

Century, J., Cassata, A., & Leslie, D. (2018, April 14)
Implementing standards initiatives in mathematics and science within a large, urban district: Principal perspectives on supports and barriers. Paper presented at the American Educational Research Association Annual Meeting, New York, NY.

Clotfelter, C.T., Ladd, H.F., & Vigdor J.L. (2015)
The aftermath of accelerating algebra evidence from district policy initiatives. *Journal of Human Resources, 50*(1), 159-188.

College Board. (2015)
Test specifications for the redesigned SAT. New York, NY: The College Board.

Common Core State Standards Initiative. (2020)
Standards for mathematical practice. Retrieved from http://www.corestandards.org/Math/Practice/

Desimone, L.M., Stornaiuolo, A., Flores, N., Pak, K., Edgerton, A., Nichols, T.P., Plummer, E.C. & Porter, A. (2019)
Success and challenges of the "new" college-and-career ready standards. Seven implementation trends. *Educational Researcher, 48*(3), 167-178.

Downey, M. (2018, January 16)
Betsy DeVos: Common Core is dead at U.S. Department of Education. *The Atlanta Journal-Constitution.* Retrieved from https://www.ajc.com/blog/get-schooled/betsy-devos-common-core-dead-department-education/cQzYu1G-8fauL6KPp41aVgJ/

Friedrichsen, P.J., & Barnett, E. (2018)
Negotiating the meaning of Next Generation Science Standards in a secondary biology teacher professional learning community. *Research in Science Teaching, 55*(7), 999-1025.

Gamoran, A., & Hannigan, E.C. (2000)
Algebra for everyone? Benefits of college-preparatory mathematics for students with diverse abilities in early secondary school. *Educational Evaluation and Policy Analysis, 22*(3), 241-254.

Gwynne, J.A., & Cowhy, J.R., (2017)
Getting ready for the Common Core State Standards: Experiences of CPS teachers and administrators preparing for the new standards. Chicago, IL: University of Chicago Consortium on School Research.

Haag, S., & Megowan, C. (2015)
Next Generation Science Standards: A national mixed-methods study on teacher readiness. *School Science and Mathematics, 115*(8), 416-426.

Hamilton, L.S., Kaufman, J.H., Stecher, B.M., Naftel, S., Robbins, M., Thompson, L.R., Garber, C., Faxon-Mills, S., & Opfer, D.O. (2016)
What supports do teachers need to help students meet Common Core State Standards for Mathematics? Findings from the American Teacher and American School Leader Panels. Santa Monica, CA: RAND Corporation.

Hatch, T. (2013)
Beneath the surface of accountability: Answerability, responsibility, and capacity-building in recent education reforms in Norway. *Journal of Educational Change, 14*(2), 113-138.

Hess, F.M. (1998)
The urban reform paradox. *American School Board Journal, 185*(2), 24-27.

Kane, T.J., Owens, A.M., Marinell, W.H., Thal, D.R.C., & Staiger, D.O. (2016)
Teaching higher: Educators' perspectives on Common Core implementation. Cambridge, MA: Cambridge Center for Education Policy Research, Harvard University.

Makkonen, R., & Sheffield, R. (2016)
California standards implementation: Presentation to the California State Board of Education. San Francisco, CA: WestEd.

MARS. (2012)
Balanced assessment in mathematics. Retrieved from https://www.mathshell.org/ba_mars.htm

O'Day, J.A., & Smith, M.S. (2016)
Quality and equality in American education: Systematic problems, systematic solutions. In I. Kirsch & H. Braun (Eds.), *The dynamics of opportunity in America* (pp. 297-358). New York, NY: Springer.

Opfer, V.D., Kaufman, J.H., & Thompson, L.E., (2016)
Implementation of k-12 state standards for mathematics and English language arts and literacy: Findings from the American Teacher Panel. Santa Monica, CA: RAND Corporation.

Polikoff, M.S., & Porter, A.C. (2014)
Instructional alignment as a measure of teaching quality. *Educational Evaluation and Policy Analysis, 36*(4), 399-416.

Scholastic & the Bill and Melinda Gates Foundation. (2014)
Teachers' views on the Common Core State Standards one year later. Retrieved from https://www.scholastic.com/primarysources/PrimarySources-2014update.pdf

Shernoff, D.J., Sinha, S., Bressler, D.M., & Schultz, D., (2017)
Teacher perception of their curricular and pedagogical shifts: Outcomes of a project-based model of teacher professional development in the next generation science standards. *Frontiers in Psychology, 8,* 989.

Simzar, R., Domina, T., & Tran, C. (2016)
Eighth-grade algebra course placement and student motivation for mathematics. *AERA Open, 2*(1), 1-26.

Sporte, S.E., Correa, M., Hart, H.M., & Wechsler, M.E. (2009)
High school reform in Chicago Public Schools: Instructional development systems. Chicago, IL: University of Chicago Consortium on Chicago School Research.

Swars, S.L., & Chestnut, C. (2016)
Transitioning to the Common Core State Standards for Mathematics: A mixed methods study of elementary teachers' experiences and Perspectives. *School Science and Mathematics, 116*(4), 212-224.

Tekkumru-Kisa, M., Schunn, C., Stein, M.K., & Reynolds, B. (2019)
Change in thinking demands for students across the phases of a science task: An exploratory study. *Research in Science Education, 49*(3), 859-883.

Toch, T. (1991)
In the name of excellence: The struggle to reform the nation's schools, why it's failing, and what should be done. Cary, NC: Oxford University Press.

Tyack, D., & Cuban, L. (1995)
Tinkering toward utopia: A century of public school reform. Cambridge, MA: Harvard University Press.

Tyler, B., Britton, T., Iveland, A., Nguyen, K., & Hipps, J. (2018)
Engaged and learning science: How students benefit from Next Generation Science Standards teaching. San Francisco, CA: WestEd.

Windschitl, M.A., & Stroupe, D. (2017)
The three-story challenge: Implications of the next generation science standards for teacher preparation. *Journal of Teacher Education, 68*(3), 251-261.

Standards-Driven Instructional Improvement: Lessons Learned in Chicago

SUPPLEMENTAL APPENDIX MAY 2022

This document provides further details about the information shared in <u>the corresponding report</u> and journal articles for readers who would like additional information:[1]

1. **Data from teacher surveys** about how they used district resources for the Common Core State Standards (CCSS) and Next Generation Science Standards (NGSS), answering the questions:

   a. To what extent did teachers report using different types of supports for standards implementation in the districtwide surveys?

   b. How were the use of instructional resources in math related to the frequency with which teachers reported using standards-aligned practices?

2. **Figures that show how the district's implementation influenced equity in math experiences and outcomes,** information that is difficult to discern—or not available—from the tables in the journal articles and main report. These figures answer questions such as:

   a. To what extent did instructional practices change for students with low initial test scores vs. those with high initial test scores in schools with more professional development around the standards?

   b. To what extent did instructional practices change for students, based on the socioeconomic resources in students' communities?

3. **A more comprehensive analysis of the relationship between teacher and student reports of instructional practices at their schools and student gains on assessments** than was practical in the journal article, answering the question: How were student test score gains in math related to the school-wide instructional practices reported by students and teachers?

4. **Longer definitions of teacher-leader practices and school supports** than described in the main report.

---

[1] Allensworth, Cashdollar, & Gwynne (2021); Cassata & Allensworth (2021); Allensworth, Cashdollar, & Cassata (2022); Century, Cassata, & Leslie (2018).

1.A: To what extent did teachers report using different types of supports for standards implementation in the districtwide surveys?

Teacher reports on the 2017–18 *5Essentials* Survey aligned with the structure of the district plan, with the use of a teacher-leader model to build stronger instructional practices, and stronger use of resources curated at the district's Knowledge Center. The most frequent sources of professional learning came from interactions with school colleagues (**see Figures A.1. and A.2**). In both the middle grades and the high school grades, and in both math and science, many teachers reported frequently participating in collaborative planning time and classroom observations with other teachers. The district emphasis on instructional practices was also evident in teachers' survey reports of the content of their professional learning around the standards, with more teachers reporting that "developing high-quality instructional practice" was substantially emphasized over other topics (**see Figures A.3 and A.4**).

FIGURE A.1

Math Teacher Participation in Professional Learning around the Standards

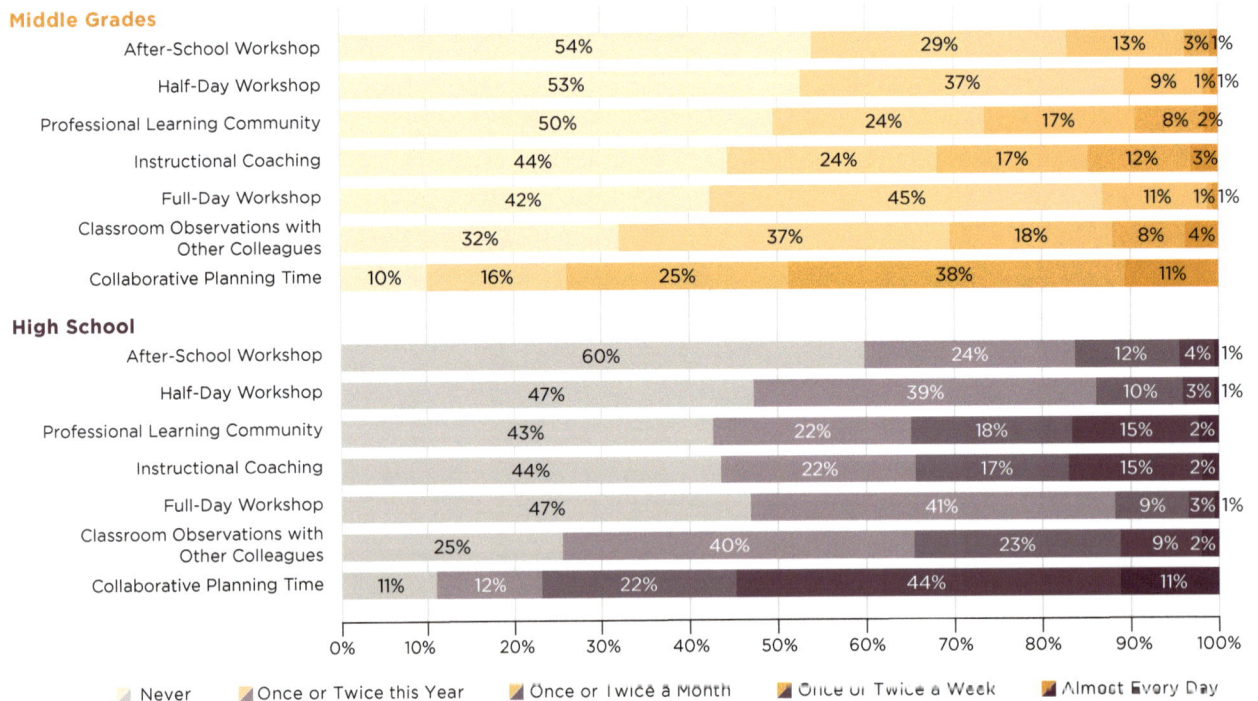

Note: Based on 1,723 middle grade and 919 high school teachers responding to questions about CCSS-M implementation in the spring 2018 survey. Component rates, as labeled, may not sum to 100 due to rounding.

Science Teacher Participation in Professional Learning around the Standards

Middle Grades

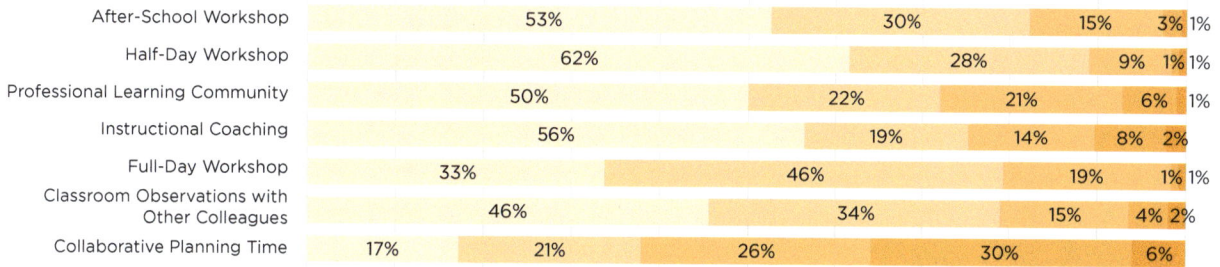

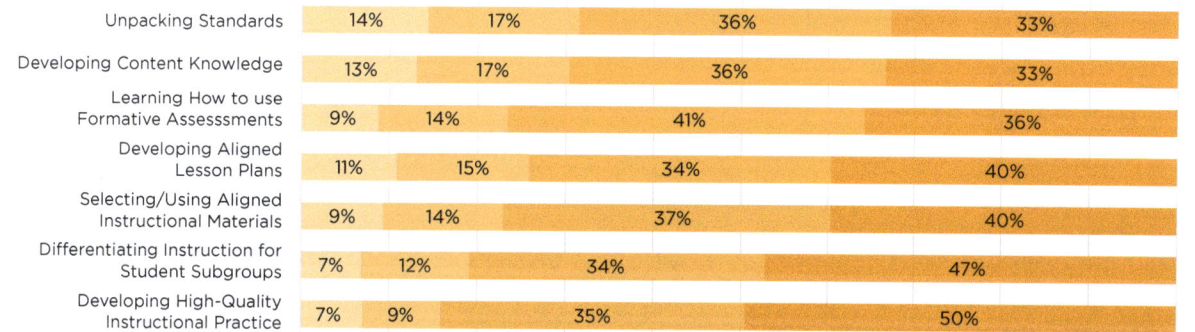

	Never	Once or Twice this Year	Once or Twice a Month	Once or Twice a Week	Almost Every Day
After-School Workshop	53%	30%	15%	3%	1%
Half-Day Workshop	62%	28%	9%	1%	1%
Professional Learning Community	50%	22%	21%	6%	1%
Instructional Coaching	56%	19%	14%	8%	2%
Full-Day Workshop	33%	46%	19%	1%	1%
Classroom Observations with Other Colleagues	46%	34%	15%	4%	2%
Collaborative Planning Time	17%	21%	26%	30%	6%

High School

	Never	Once or Twice this Year	Once or Twice a Month	Once or Twice a Week	Almost Every Day
After-School Workshop	57%	22%	17%	4%	2%
Half-Day Workshop	47%	36%	13%	2%	1%
Professional Learning Community	42%	21%	21%	12%	4%
Instructional Coaching	41%	19%	21%	16%	3%
Full-Day Workshop	43%	42%	12%	1%	1%
Classroom Observations with Other Colleagues	24%	35%	27%	10%	4%
Collaborative Planning Time	8%	12%	23%	41%	16%

Legend: Never | Once or Twice this Year | Once or Twice a Month | Once or Twice a Week | Almost Every Day

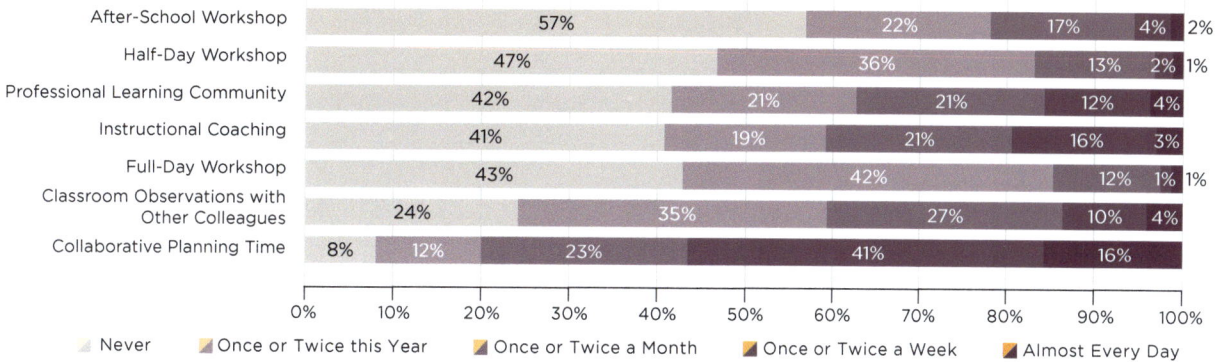

Note: Based on 782 middle grade and 685 high school teachers responding to questions about NGSS implementation in the spring 2018 survey. Component rates, as labeled, may not sum to 100 due to rounding.

Math Teacher Reports of the Emphasis of their Professional Development around the CCSS-M

Middle Grades

	Was Not Addressed	Minimal Emphasis	Moderate Emphasis	Major Emphasis
Unpacking Standards	14%	17%	36%	33%
Developing Content Knowledge	13%	17%	36%	33%
Learning How to use Formative Assessments	9%	14%	41%	36%
Developing Aligned Lesson Plans	11%	15%	34%	40%
Selecting/Using Aligned Instructional Materials	9%	14%	37%	40%
Differentiating Instruction for Student Subgroups	7%	12%	34%	47%
Developing High-Quality Instructional Practice	7%	9%	35%	50%

High School

	Was Not Addressed	Minimal Emphasis	Moderate Emphasis	Major Emphasis
Unpacking Standards	16%	22%	35%	27%
Developing Content Knowledge	21%	23%	34%	22%
Learning How to use Formative Assessments	11%	17%	43%	29%
Developing Aligned Lesson Plans	15%	20%	38%	28%
Selecting/Using Aligned Instructional Materials	11%	19%	41%	28%
Differentiating Instruction for Student Subgroups	13%	19%	38%	30%
Developing High-Quality Instructional Practice	10%	13%	40%	37%

Legend: Was Not Addressed | Minimal Emphasis | Moderate Emphasis | Major Emphasis

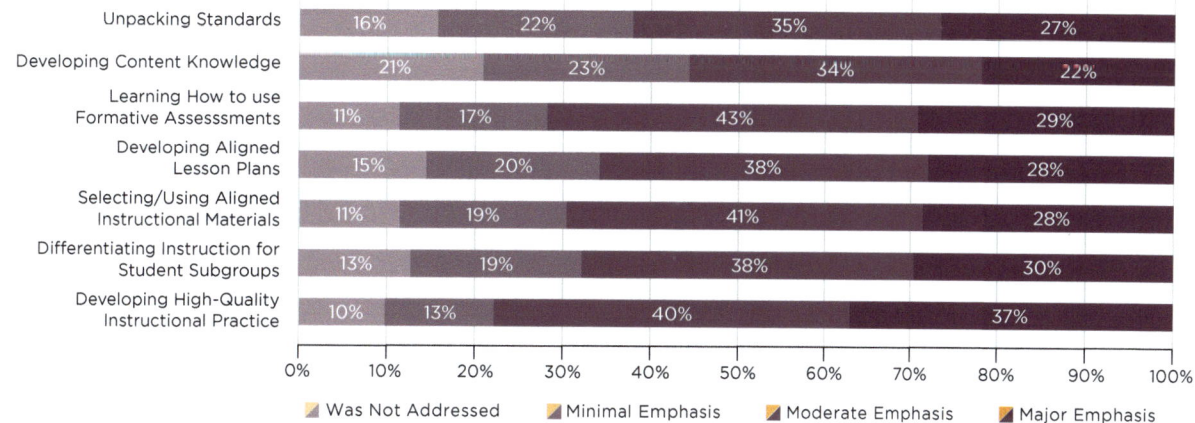

Note: Based on 1,723 middle grade and 919 high school teachers responding to questions about CCSS-M implementation in the spring 2018 survey. Component rates, as labeled, may not sum to 100 due to rounding.

Science Teacher Reports of the Emphasis of their Professional Development around the NGSS

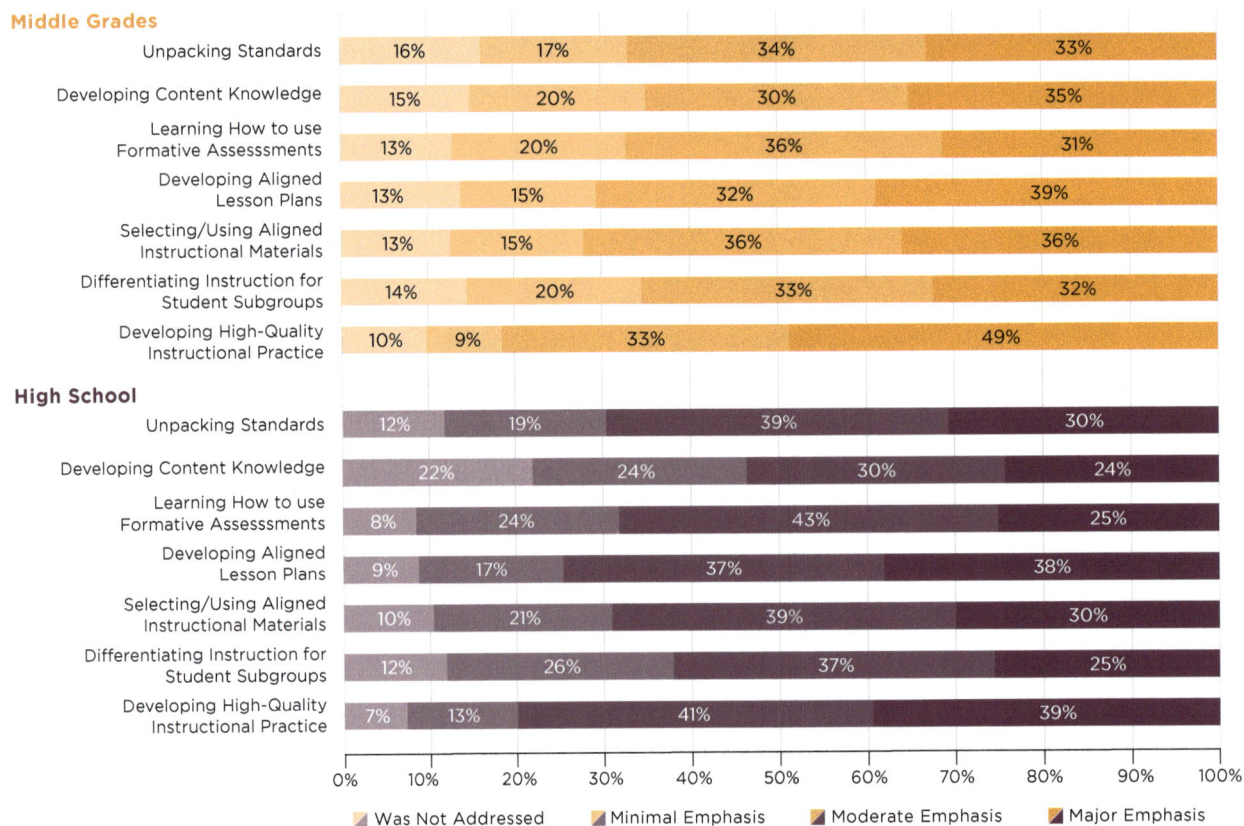

Middle Grades

	Was Not Addressed	Minimal Emphasis	Moderate Emphasis	Major Emphasis
Unpacking Standards	16%	17%	34%	33%
Developing Content Knowledge	15%	20%	30%	35%
Learning How to use Formative Assesssments	13%	20%	36%	31%
Developing Aligned Lesson Plans	13%	15%	32%	39%
Selecting/Using Aligned Instructional Materials	13%	15%	36%	36%
Differentiating Instruction for Student Subgroups	14%	20%	33%	32%
Developing High-Quality Instructional Practice	10%	9%	33%	49%

High School

	Was Not Addressed	Minimal Emphasis	Moderate Emphasis	Major Emphasis
Unpacking Standards	12%	19%	39%	30%
Developing Content Knowledge	22%	24%	30%	24%
Learning How to use Formative Assesssments	8%	24%	43%	25%
Developing Aligned Lesson Plans	9%	17%	37%	38%
Selecting/Using Aligned Instructional Materials	10%	21%	39%	30%
Differentiating Instruction for Student Subgroups	12%	26%	37%	25%
Developing High-Quality Instructional Practice	7%	13%	41%	39%

Was Not Addressed — Minimal Emphasis — Moderate Emphasis — Major Emphasis

Note: Based on 782 middle grade and 685 high school teachers responding to questions about NGSS implementation in the spring 2018 survey. Component rates, as labeled, may not sum to the total rate due to rounding.

1.B: How were the use of instructional resources in math related to the frequency with which teachers reported using standards-aligned practices?

Math professional development encouraged the use of MARS tasks and Math Talks to facilitate standards-aligned practices. On the 2017–18 *5Essentials* Survey, teachers who reported more frequently using either MARS tasks or Math Talks also were more likely to report engaging in standards-aligned practices: having students discuss different ways to approach a problem, engaging in problems that allowed for multiple solutions, and having students justify their reasoning in writing (**see Figure A.5**). For example, 96 percent of teachers who used Math Talks two or more times a week also reported asking their students to discuss different ways to approach a problem two or more times a week. The relationships were stronger in the middle grades than in the high school grades; high school teachers were much less likely than middle grade teachers to use either resource.

Teachers Who Used Math Talks and MARS Tasks Resources More Often Engaged in More Standards-Aligned Practices

*How often students **discussed ways to approach a problem** by use of...*

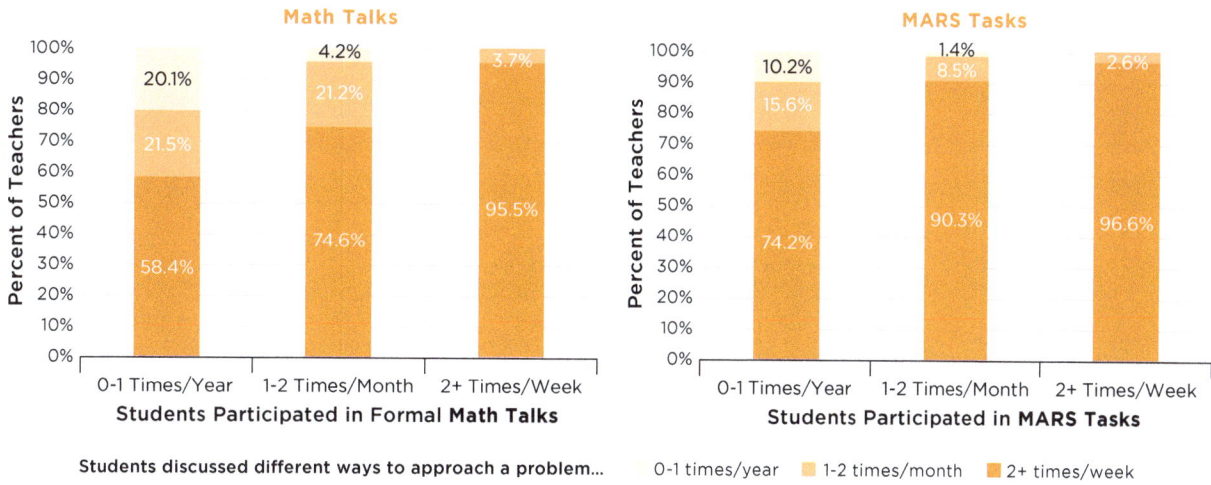

Students discussed different ways to approach a problem... ▢ 0-1 times/year ▢ 1-2 times/month ▢ 2+ times/week

*How often students **justified their reason in writing** by use of...*

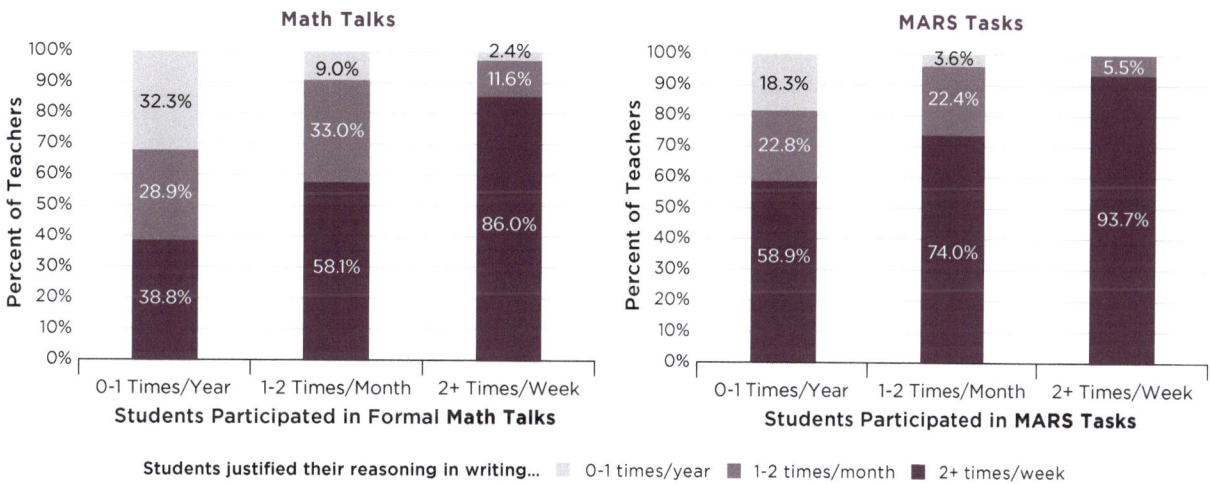

Students justified their reasoning in writing... ▢ 0-1 times/year ▢ 1-2 times/month ▢ 2+ times/week

*How often students **engaged in a problem that allowed for multiple solution methods** by use of...*

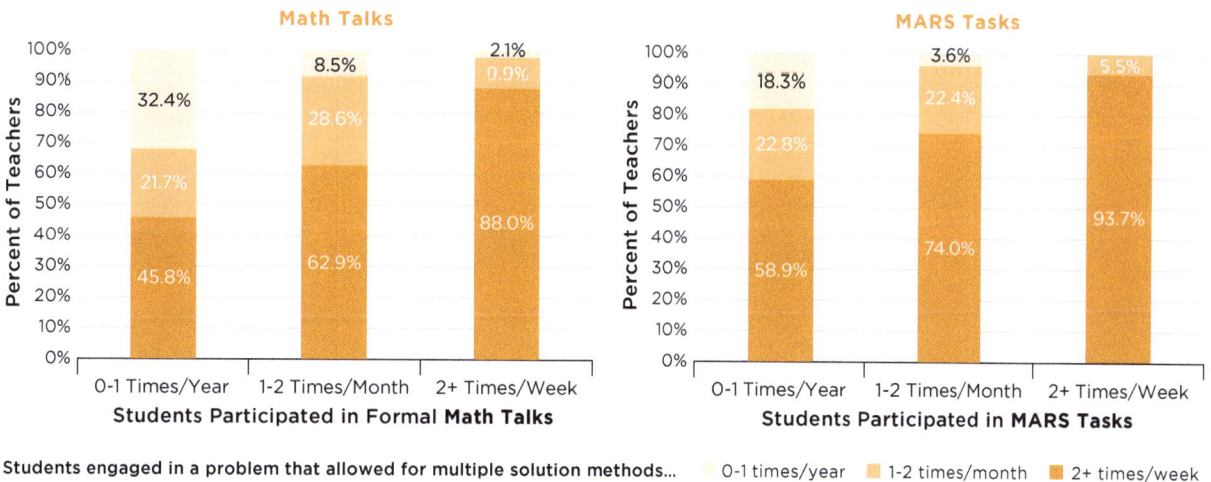

Students engaged in a problem that allowed for multiple solution methods... ▢ 0-1 times/year ▢ 1-2 times/month ▢ 2+ times/week

Note: Based on the responses of mathematics teachers to questions in the 2018 spring survey. Component rates, as labeled, may not sum to 100 due to rounding.

2.A: To what extent did instructional practices change for students with low initial test scores vs. high initial test scores in schools with more professional development around the standards?

Before standards implementation, students with high test scores reported using standards-aligned instructional practices significantly more often in their math classes than students with low test scores. As shown in **Figure A.6**, in 2010–11, student reports on the math instructional practices measure were about 0.3 standard deviations higher among students with high test scores than students with low test scores, with similar differences in schools that subsequently took up extensive professional learning around the standards as those that had more limited professional learning. Students with low test scores experienced improvements in math instruction over the next several years, with the biggest improvement occurring in 2014–15, the year the standards were implemented. By the 2016–17 school year, there had been improvements in the frequency of students' experiences with standards-aligned practices among both high- and low-testing students at schools with extensive professional learning, but the changes were largest for students who had low tested skills, relative to students at the same schools in prior years. Furthermore, in 2016–17, the reports of students with low test scores at the schools that had extensive professional learning around the standards in 2014–15 were higher than the reports of students with high test scores at the schools with limited professional learning around the standards.

FIGURE A.6

Changes in Students' Reports of Instructional Practices in Middle Grades Math by Teachers' Reports of their Professional Learning around the Standards in 2014–15

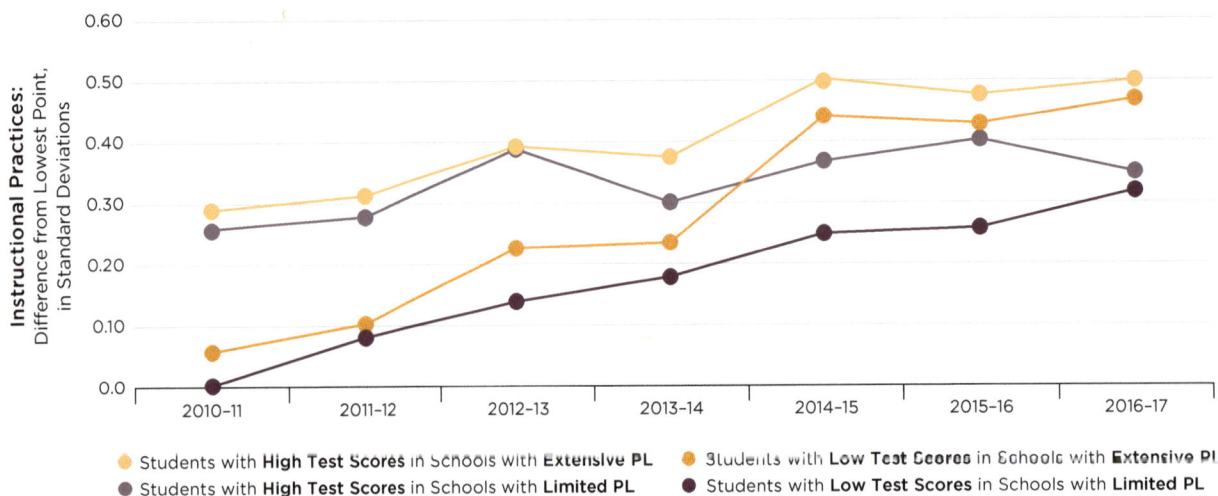

Legend:
- Students with **High Test Scores** in Schools with **Extensive PL**
- Students with **Low Test Scores** in Schools with **Extensive PL**
- Students with **High Test Scores** in Schools with **Limited PL**
- Students with **Low Test Scores** in Schools with **Limited PL**

Note: Students were divided into groups based on ISAT or PARCC math scores in the prior year; students with high test scores were at least 0.5 standard deviations above the mean, while students with low test scores were at least 0.5 standard deviations below the mean. Values for 2014–15 come from regression models that control for student race, ethnicity, gender, neighborhood poverty level, neighborhood socioeconomic status, the type/s of math class in which the student was enrolled, and math score on the state assessment in the prior spring. Changes relative to 2013–14 are based on coefficients from models with school and year fixed-effects and the same covariates. The school fixed effects control for any differences in 2013–14 among schools attended by different students. Teacher reports of professional learning come from the 2014–15 teacher survey and are based on questions about how frequently they engaged in different types of professional learning around the standards. See Allensworth, Cashdollar, and Gwynne (2021) for more details.

2.B: To what extent did instructional practices change for students based on the socioeconomic resources in students' communities?

Students from all types of neighborhoods reported more frequently engaging in standards-aligned practices in their math classes in 2017–18 than 2011–21 **(see Figure A.7)**. In elementary schools, improvement was especially large in the year the standards were to be fully implemented, 2014–15, with the largest changes coming in schools that served students living in neighborhoods with the fewest socioeconomic resources.

FIGURE A.7

Changes in Math Instructional Practices Were Largest in Schools Serving Students Living in Neighborhoods with the Fewest Socioeconomic Resources

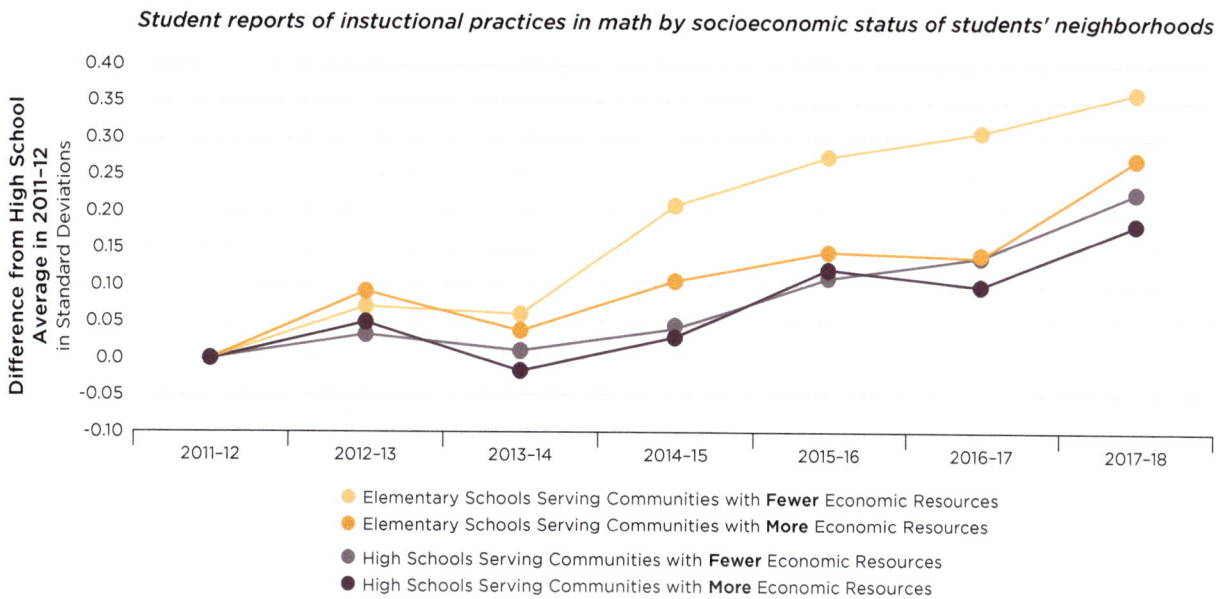

Student reports of instuctional practices in math by socioeconomic status of students' neighborhoods

Legend:
- Elementary Schools Serving Communities with **Fewer** Economic Resources
- Elementary Schools Serving Communities with **More** Economic Resources
- High Schools Serving Communities with **Fewer** Economic Resources
- High Schools Serving Communities with **More** Economic Resources

Note: Community socioeconomic resources are based on the characteristics of students' residential neighborhoods: percentage of families below the poverty line and male unemployment, aggregated to the school level. Schools serving communities with more socioeconomic resources are in the lowest one-third of schools; schools serving communities with fewer resources are in the highest one-third of schools.

3. How were student test score gains in math related to the school-wide instructional practices reported by students and teachers?

To discern the relationships between teacher or student reports of instructional practices and students' test score gains, we used 2-level hierarchical linear models predicting students' gains on assessments at the student level with instructional practices at the school level. Instructional practices were calculated as the average of either teacher or student reports in the school in 2017–18. At the student level, we predicted each student's test score with their prior year score, as well as covariates for gender, race, IEP status, neighborhood poverty, and socioeconomic status. At the school level, we included variables for school average teacher/student reports of instructional practices, as well as school average test scores in the prior year, average socioeconomic status, and poverty levels of students, and school racial composition. Student and school covariates were included to be certain that the relationships were not influenced by any differences in the use of practices across schools serving students with different backgrounds or achievement levels. We also ran the analyses separately based on students' prior year achievement, with students divided into three equal groups, based on their prior scores. The models took the form:

$$2018\text{Score}_{ij} = \beta_{0j} + \beta_{1j}(2017\text{Score})_{ij} + \sum_{c=2}^{8} \beta_{cj}\text{StuCov}_{ij} + e_{ij}$$

$$\beta_{0j} = \gamma_{00} + \gamma_{01}(\text{Instructional Practices})_j + \sum_{s=2}^{6} \gamma_s \text{SchlCov}_j + r_j$$

At the student level, the 2017–18 test score is modeled as a function of their prior year score, along with their gender, race, neighborhood poverty, socioeconomic status, and IEP status. β_{0j} represents the average gain in the school, controlling for student background characteristics. β_{0j} is predicted at level 2 with the measure of average reports of instructional practices, along with school-level covariates controlling for average prior year achievement, average poverty, and socioeconomic status of students, and school racial composition. γ_{01} provides the relationship of instructional practices with student average gains, net of any relationship of gains with the school covariates. Only the intercept is allowed to vary at the school level.

The results are shown in **Figure A.8** for the analyses that separated students into three groups based on their prior test scores. Each set of bars shows the difference in gains for a given achievement group in a given grade if at a school with frequent use of standards-aligned practices versus an average school in the district. The first group of bars for each grade uses student reports of instructional practices at the school as the independent variable, while the second group of bars uses teacher reports. Only relationships that are statistically significant are included. For students with low and average prior achievement, there were significant relationships between student reports of instructional practices at the school and test gains in grades 6-9, and with teacher reports there were significant relationships in grades 6-8, and in ninth grade for students with low test scores. For students with high prior achievement scores, the relationships between instructional practices and students' gains on math tests were nonsignificant at all middle grade levels, and only significantly related to student reports in ninth grade.

Differences in Math Gains Relative to the District Average in Schools with Frequent Use of Standards-Aligned Practices, by Prior Student Achievement

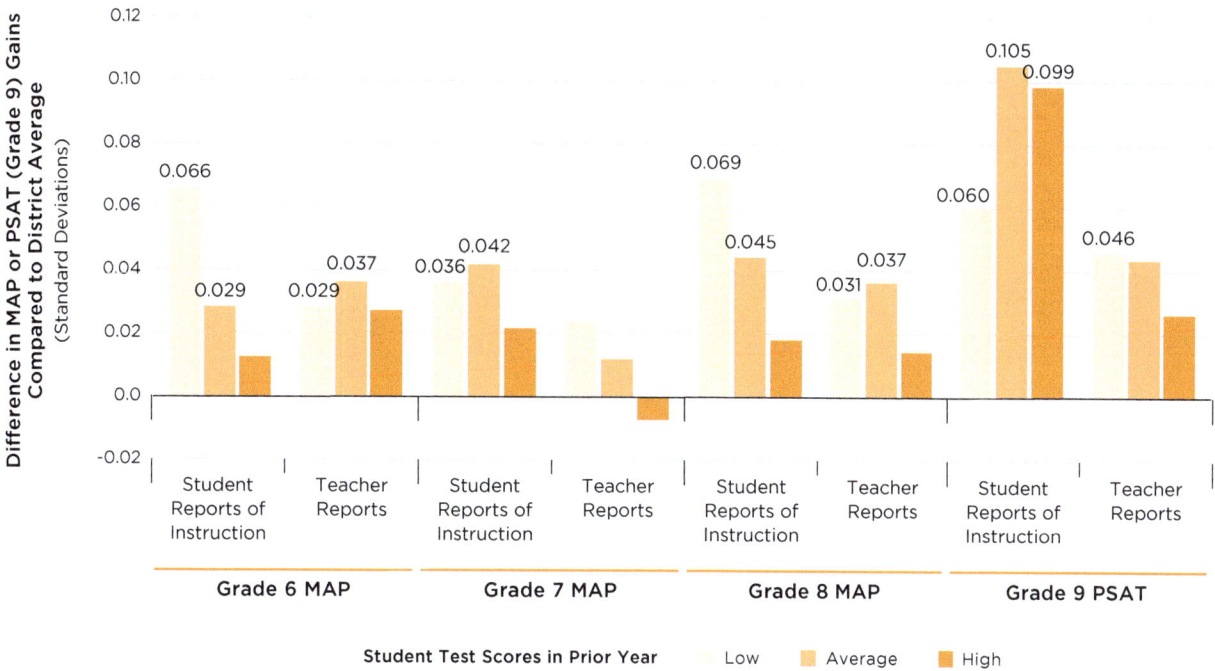

Note: Bars with labels indicate gains that are significantly different from average at p<0.05 (most are significant at p<0.01). Schools with stronger standards-aligned practices are one standard deviation above the mean in terms of either student reports of practices in the school or teacher reports of practices in the school. Student survey reports are based on about 80 percent of students in a given grade level in the district, while teacher reports are based on about 60 percent of math teachers in the district. Gains are based on the 2018 NWEA-MAP in grades 6-8 and the PSAT in grades 9-10. Models control for student's score in the same subject test the prior year, with the exception of ninth grade where the student's eighth-grade NWEA-MAP score in math is used as the prior score. The models also control for students' race, ethnicity, socioeconomic background, special education status, and school economic composition (mean poverty and mean social status), school racial composition, and average test scores in the prior year.

4. Definitions of teacher-leader practices and school supports.

Teacher leaders described the practices they used to encourage greater use of standards-aligned instruction in their schools, as well as the supports that enabled them to more effectively support instructional change in their schools. Five practices and five supports emerged as important, based on interviews with 16 teacher leaders (seven in math and nine in science), representing 13 CPS schools located across Chicago.

TABLE A.1

Five Teacher Leader Practices and Descriptions

Advocating for Change	Works with school leadership to establish systems and monitor progress that support instructional change.
Providing Individual Support	Acts as a mentor; demonstrates instruction and offers suggestions about ways to change instruction.
Inspiring Others	Models an innovative practice and gets others curious to try it without the explicit intention to do so.
Sharing with Colleagues	Intentionally disseminates or exchanges information about resources and practices; such as demonstrating how to access and use standards-aligned instructional resources in the Knowledge Center.
Working in Collaboration	Works with one or more colleagues to create, test, and reflect on new resources, tools, and methods to address the new standards.

TABLE A.2

Five School Supports for Practices and Descriptions

School Administrator Support and Advocacy	**Administrators:** • Intentionally schedule time for teachers to receive school-based professional development and engage in collaborative work. • Contribute to teachers' collaborative work around standards-aligned instruction. • Support teacher leaders' professional growth.
Staff Commitment to the Change Effort	**Teachers:** • Are eager to try new instructional approaches that support standards-aligned instruction. • Believe that teaching in alignment with the new standards will improve student learning.
Trusting and Supportive Staff Relationships	**Teachers:** • Routinely engage in ongoing communication in and outside of structured meetings. • Make classroom instruction open and transparent. • Exchange ideas and resources in formal and informal settings, including on their own time, if necessary.
Dedicated Collaboration Time	**School:** • Provides dedicated time during the school day for teacher-led teams and committees to regularly meet. • Has established structures for peer observation and feedback.
Knowledgeable Colleagues	**Teachers:** • Are familiar with standards-aligned instruction. • Have begun making instructional shifts in alignment with new standards. • Are engaged in school initiatives that support standards-aligned instruction.

ABOUT THE AUTHORS

ELAINE M. ALLENSWORTH is the Lewis-Sebring Director of the UChicago Consortium, where she has conducted research on educational policy and practice for the last 20 years. She works with policymakers and practitioners to bridge research and practice, providing advice to researchers across the country about conducting research-practice partnerships, and serving on panels, policy commissions, and working groups at the local, state and national level. She was once a high school Spanish and science teacher.

SARAH CASHDOLLAR is the Associate Director of Research at the Illinois Workforce and Education Research Collaborative (IWERC), a research-practice partnership at the Discovery Partners Institute at the University of Illinois. Using mixed methods and a range of theoretical perspectives, she investigates reforms that aim to improve adolescent preparation for the transition from high school to postsecondary education and work.

AMY CASSATA was a Senior Research & Evaluation Scientist at Outlier Research & Evaluation at UChicago at the time this research was conducted. Her research at Outlier was devoted to understanding why educators adopt new programs, tools, and methods, measuring the extent of their use within and across settings, and determining the factors that support or deter educational change.

JULIA A. GWYNNE is a Senior Research Scientist at the UChicago Consortium, where she has conducted a number of studies examining the skills and academic behaviors students need to be ready for high school and college. She has also conducted research looking at high school graduation rates, school closings, student mobility, and preschool attendance.

JEANNE CENTURY is the Director of Outlier Research & Evaluation at UChicago STEM Education at UChicago. Over 35 years, her work has focused on advancing equity in education primarily through partnerships in urban school districts. She has received numerous grants, primarily focusing on understanding, measuring and supporting innovation implementation, spread and endurance. Jeanne has also worked on policy at local, state and federal levels and served on the Obama-Biden education transition team.

DEBBIE LESLIE is the Director of Education Outreach at UChicago STEM Education. She has 11 years of classroom teaching experience, and her work has included teaching math and science methods courses to pre-service teachers in the University of Chicago's Urban Teacher Education Program, leading the Everyday Mathematics early childhood team for the 3rd and 4th editions, developing early childhood STEM curriculum materials and programs for teachers and families, collaborating with UChicago faculty on multiple research and development projects, and designing and leading several long-term partnerships with schools focused on improving mathematics teaching and learning school-wide.

LISA SALL was the Director of Communications at the UChicago Consortium at the time this research was conducted. She collaborated with researchers and Consortium stakeholders and amplify research findings.

NICK TALLANT was a graduate student at the UChicago Harris School at the time this research was conducted. As a data scientist, policy analyst, and civic technologist with a background in music education, he enjoys breaking down problems, scaling solutions, and communicating results to people who need them.

www.ingramcontent.com/pod-product-compliance
Lightning Source LLC
Chambersburg PA
CBHW042114040426
42448CB00003B/269